ESTATE   PUE

REIGATE · MOL

DORKING · EPSOM · LEATHERH

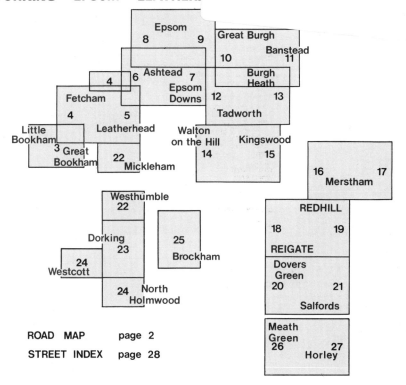

Epsom
8   9

Great Burgh
10   Banstead 11

4   6   Ashtead 7
Epsom
Downs

Fetcham

Burgh
Heath

12   13

4   5   Leatherhead

Little
Bookham
3 Great
Bookham   22 Mickleham

Walton
on the Hill   Kingswood
14   15

Tadworth

16
Merstham   17

Westhumble
22

REDHILL
18   19

Dorking
23

25
Brockham

REIGATE

24
Westcott

Dovers
Green
20   21

24   North
Holmwood

Salfords

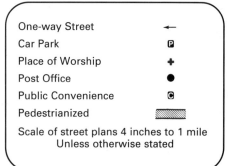

Meath
Green
26   27
Horley

Every effort has been made to verify the
accuracy of information in this book
but the publishers cannot accept
responsibility for expense or loss caused
by any error or omission. Information
that will be of assistance to the user of
the maps will be welcomed.

The representation of a road, track or
footpath on the maps in this atlas is no
evidence of the existence of a right of way.

One-way Street   ←

Car Park   P

Place of Worship   +

Post Office   ●

Public Convenience   C

Pedestrianized   ▨

Scale of street plans 4 inches to 1 mile
Unless otherwise stated

Street plans prepared and published by ESTATE PUBLICATIONS, Bridewell House,
TENTERDEN, KENT, and based upon the ORDNANCE SURVEY maps with the sanction
of the Controller of H. M. Stationery Office.

The publishers acknowledge the co-operation of the local
authorities of towns represented in this atlas.

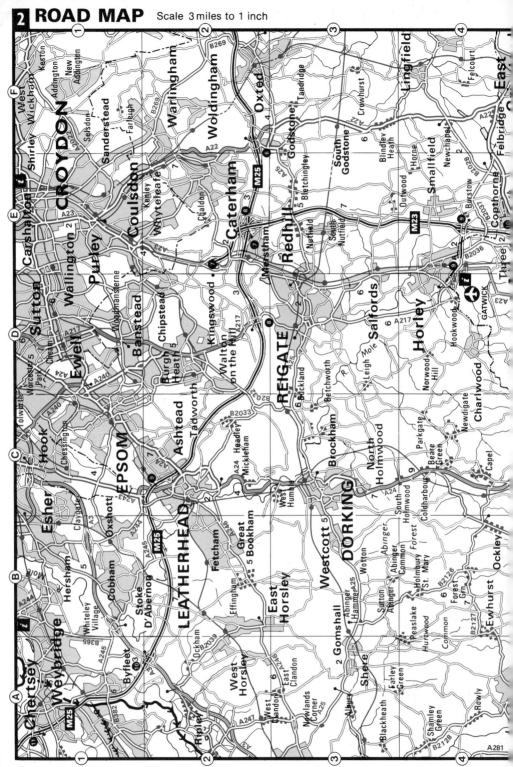

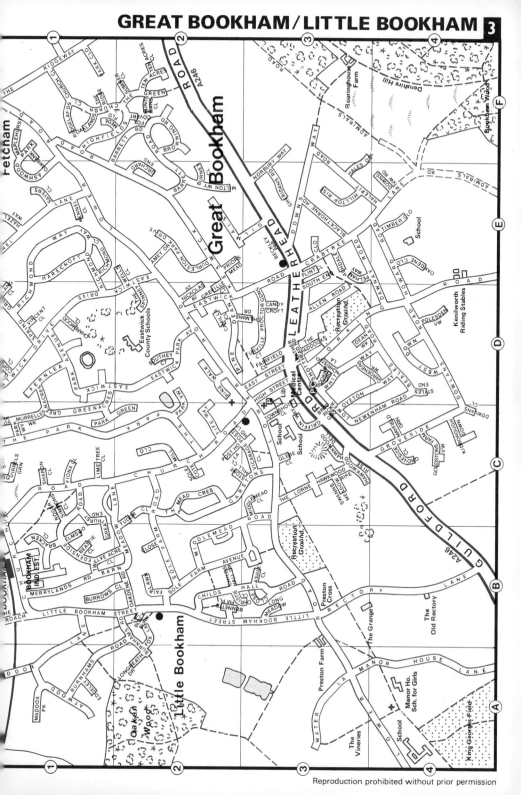

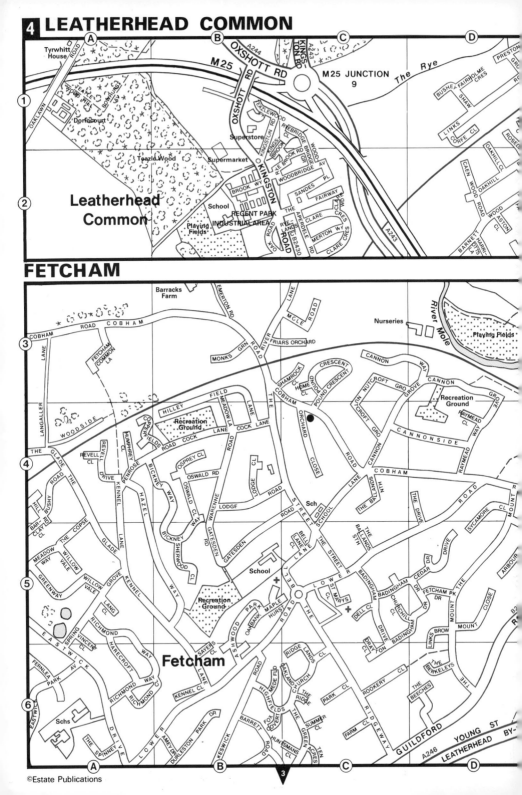

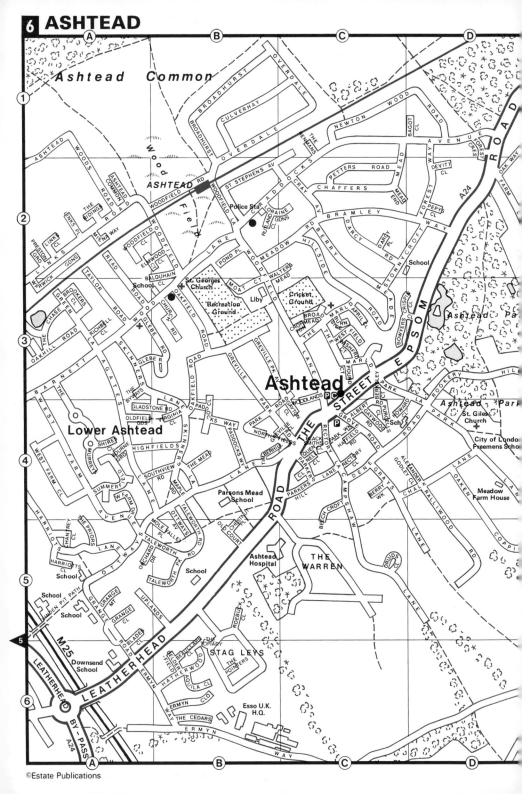

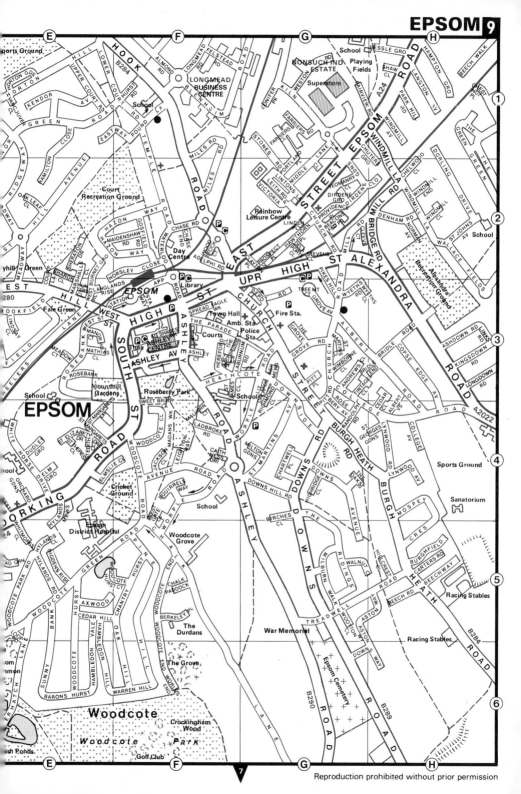

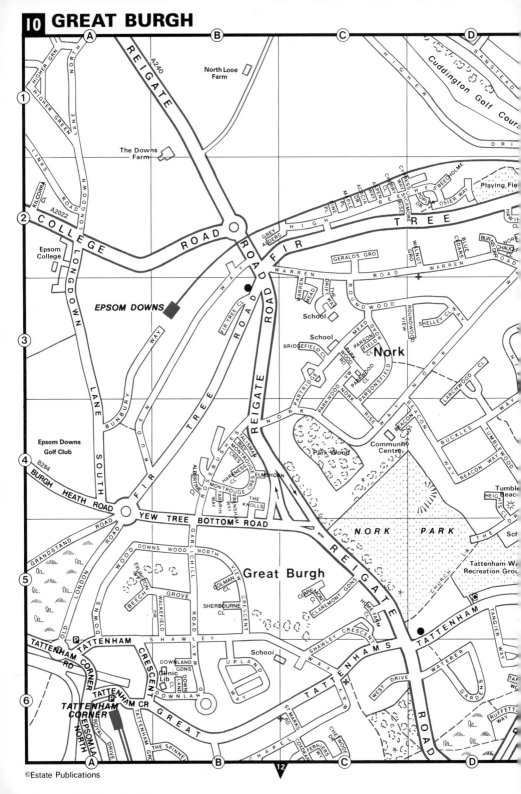

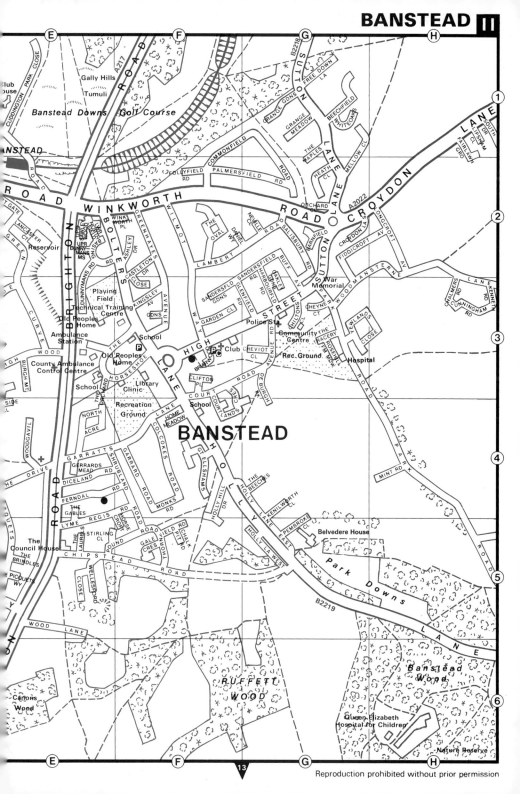

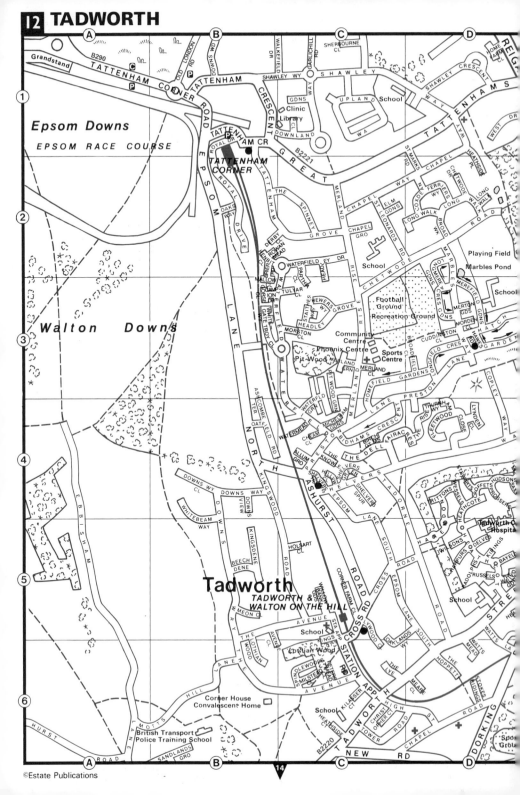

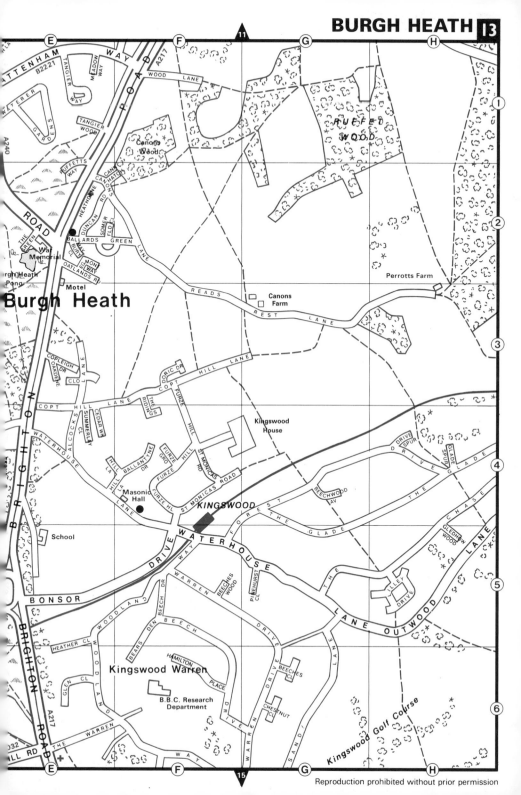

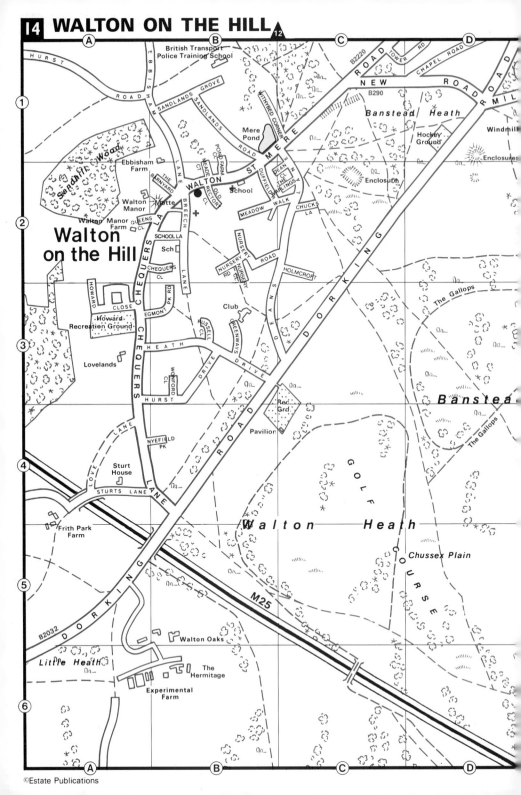

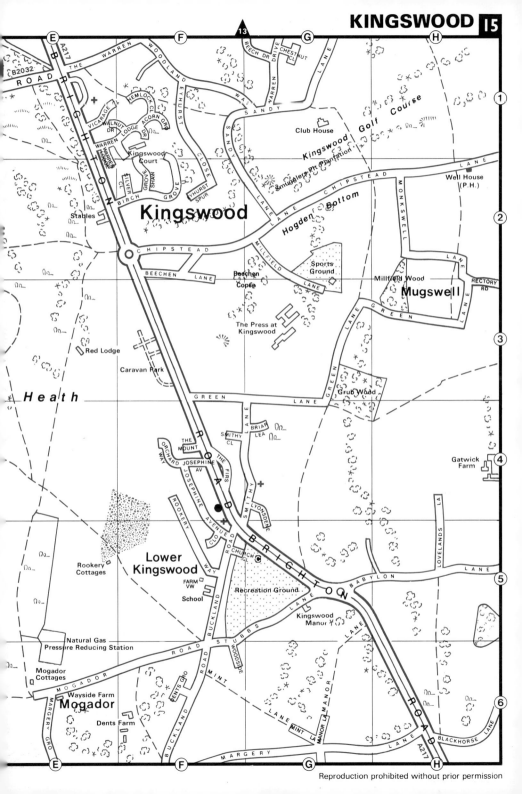

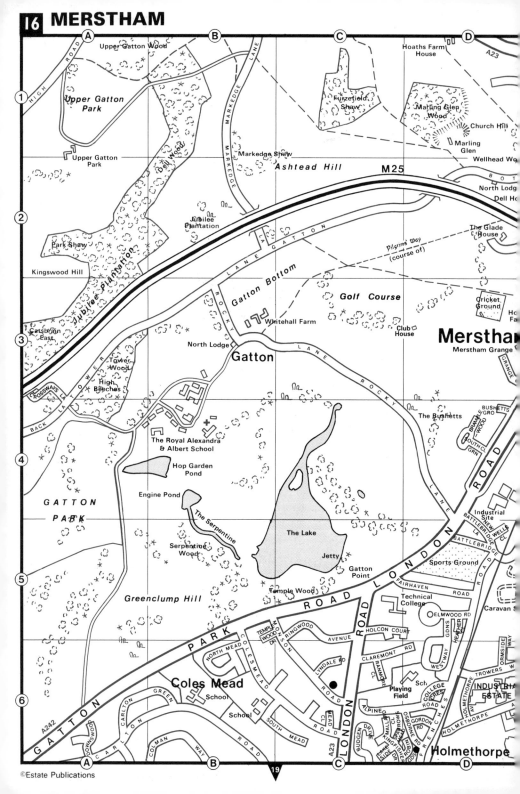

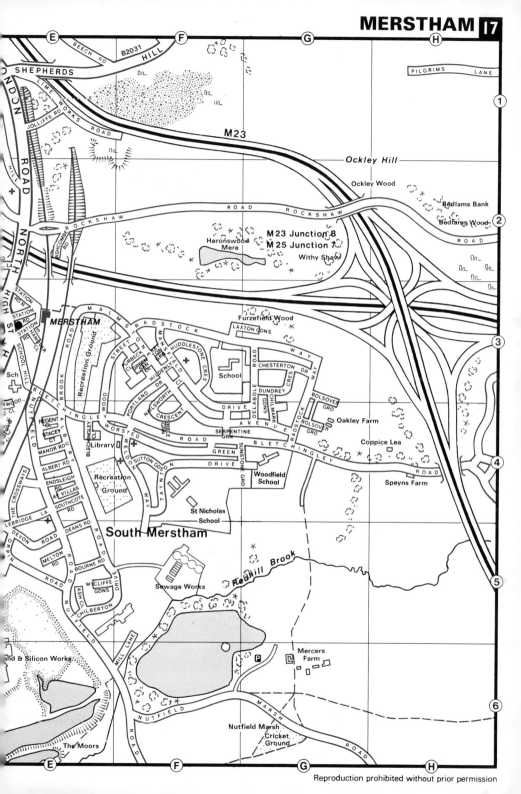

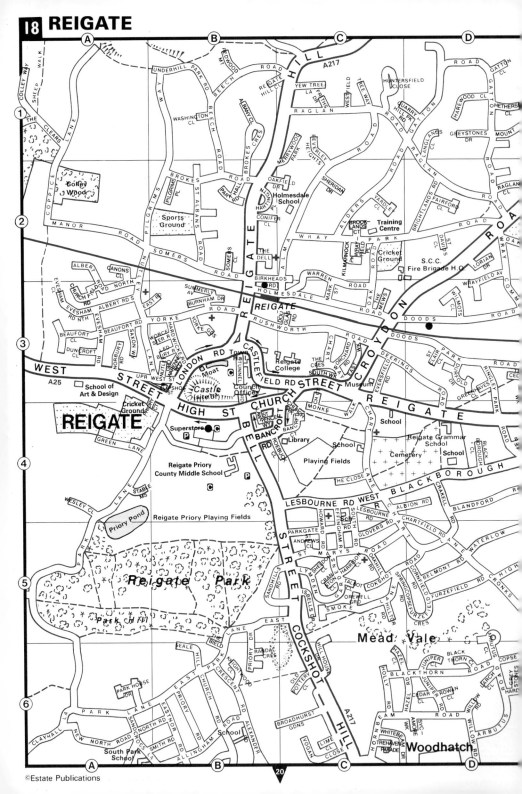

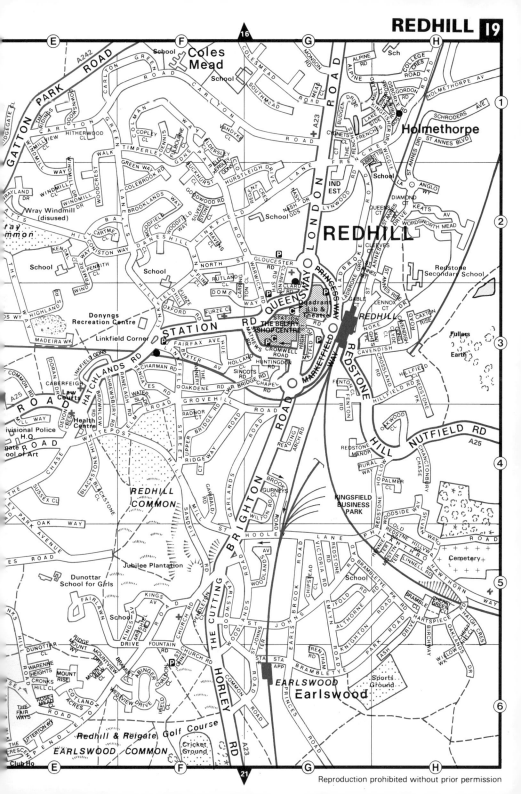

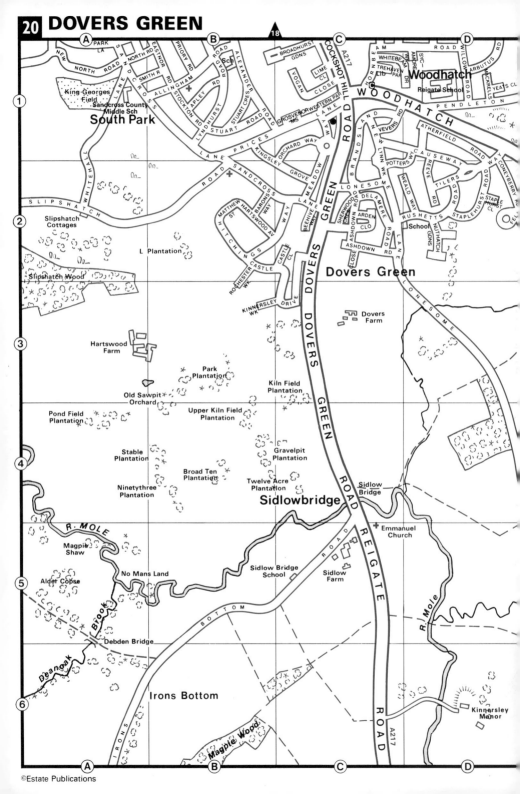

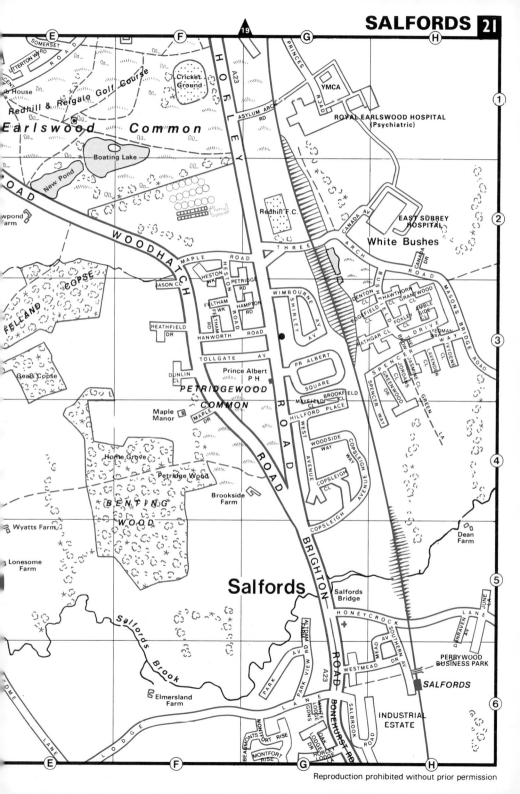

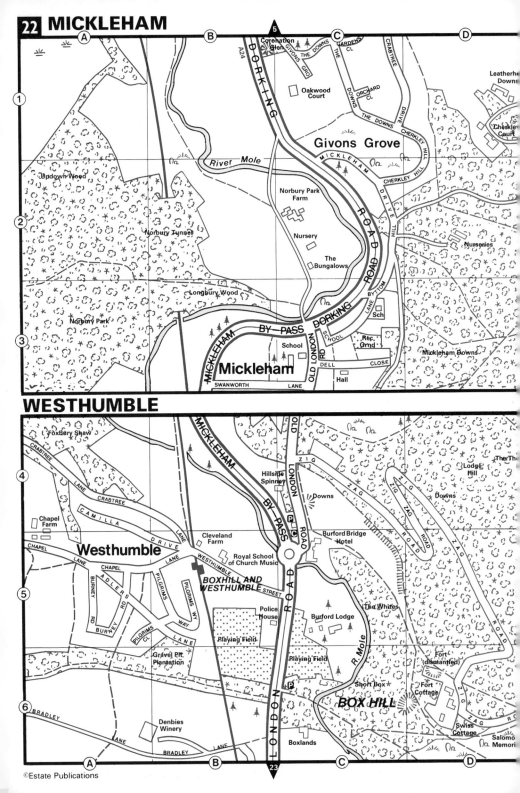

MICKLEHAM

A   B   C   D

Coronation Glen
THE DOWNS
GIVONS GRO
THE GARDENS
CL
CRABTREE CL
Leatherhe
Downs

Oakwood Court
THE DOWNS
ORCHARD CL
CHERKLEY DRIVE
Cherkley
Court

Givons Grove
River Mole
MICKLEHAM
CHERKLEY HILL
CHERKLEY HILL

Updown Wood
Norbury Park Farm
DRIVE
DORKING ROAD ROAD
Nurseries

Norbury Tunnel
Nursery
The Bungalows
BYTTOM LANE
Sch
Nurseries

Longbury Wood
SCHOOL LANE
Rec. Grnd
Mickleham Downs

Norbury Park
MICKLEHAM BY-PASS DORKING
School
OLD LONDON RD
DELL
CLOSE

Mickleham
SWANWORTH LANE
Hall

WESTHUMBLE

A   B   C   D

Foxbury Shaw
MICKLEHAM BY-PASS
OLD LONDON ROAD
ZIG
Lodge Hill
The Th

CRABTREE LANE
Hillside Spinney
ZIG
Downs
ZIG ZAG ROAD
Downs

Chapel Farm
CRABTREE LANE
CAMILLA DRIVE
Downs
ZAG ROAD

Cleveland Farm
Burford Bridge Hotel
ZIG ZAG ROAD

CHAPEL LANE
Westhumble
CHAPEL LANE
WESTHUMBLE LANE
Royal School of Church Music

BURNEY RD
ADLERS RD
PILGRIMS WY
BOXHILL AND WESTHUMBLE STREET
The Whites

BURNEY RD
PILGRIMS CL
PILGRIMS WAY LANE
Police House
Burford Lodge
ROAD

Playing Field
R. Mole
Fort (dismantled)
ZIG

Gravel Pit Plantation
Playing Field
Short Box
Fort Cottage
ZAG ROAD

BRADLEY LANE
Denbies Winery
BOX HILL
Swiss Cottage
Salomo Memori

BRADLEY LANE
Boxlands
LONDON ROAD

A   B   C   D

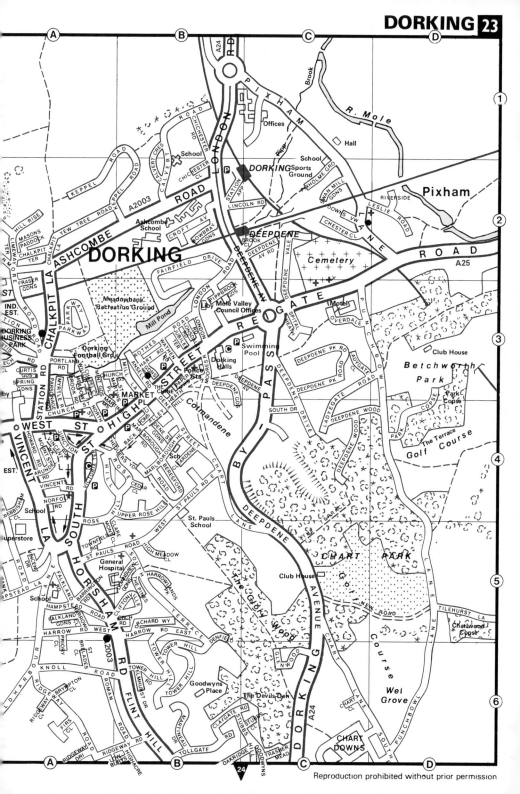

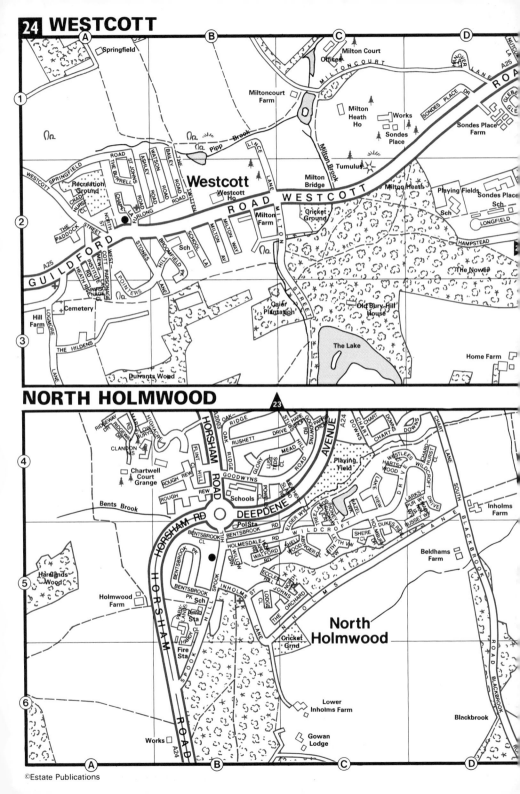

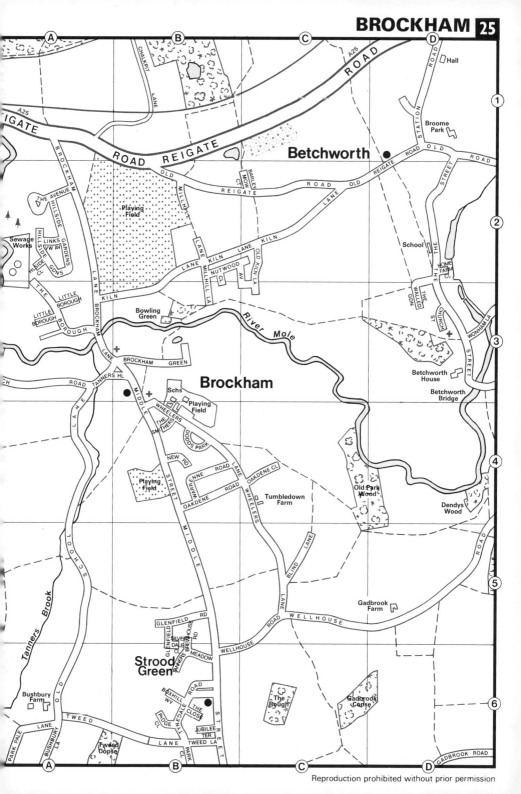

A   B   C   D

Hall

A25

ROAD

REIGATE

REIGATE ROAD

Betchworth

Broome Park

CHALKPIT LANE

THE AVENUE

HILLSIDE

BROCKHAM LANE

Sewage Works

HILLSIDE GARDENS

LINKS GARDENS

VW AV

HILLSIDE CL

Playing Field

MILLHILL

BARLEY MOW CT

OLD REIGATE ROAD

STATION ROAD

OLD STREET ROAD

School

THE WALLED GDN

HOME FARM CL

THE ST

WONHAM LA

CHURCH STREET

THE

LITTLE BOROUGH

LITTLE BOROUGH

THE BOROUGH

KILN LANE

KILN LANE

MILLHILL LA

NUTWOOD AV

OLD KILN LA

CL

Bowling Green

BROCKHAM GREEN

River Mole

Betchworth House

Betchworth Bridge

Brockham

TANNERS HL

MIDDLE

Schs

Playing Field

WHEELERS

THE SMITHERS

DODDS PARK

NEW RD

KENNE ROAD

OAKDENE

WHEELERS LANE

OAKDENE CL

Tumbledown Farm

Old Park Wood

Dendys Wood

ROAD

LANE

SCHOOL

Playing Field

STREET

MIDDLE

Tanners Brook

BLIND LANE

LANE ROAD

WELLHOUSE

Gadbrook Farm

ROAD

GLENFIELD RD

SILVER DALE

PARSONS MEAD HOUSE

MEADOW

WELLHOUSE ROAD

Strood Green

Bushbury Farm

BOXHILL WY

TYEEDALE CLOSE

RIDGE TER

STREET

THE CLOSE

The Rough

Gadbrook Copse

PARK PALE LANE

BUSHBURY LA

OLD

TWEED

JUBILEE TER

TWEED LANE

PARK CL

Tweed Copse

GADBROOK ROAD

A   B   C   D

1 2 3 4 5 6

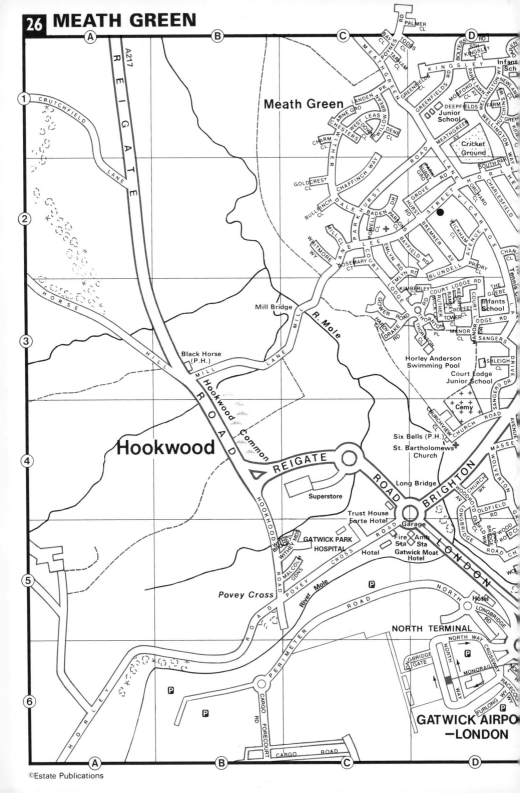

Meath Green

Hookwood

Povey Cross

NORTH TERMINAL

GATWICK AIRPO
—LONDON

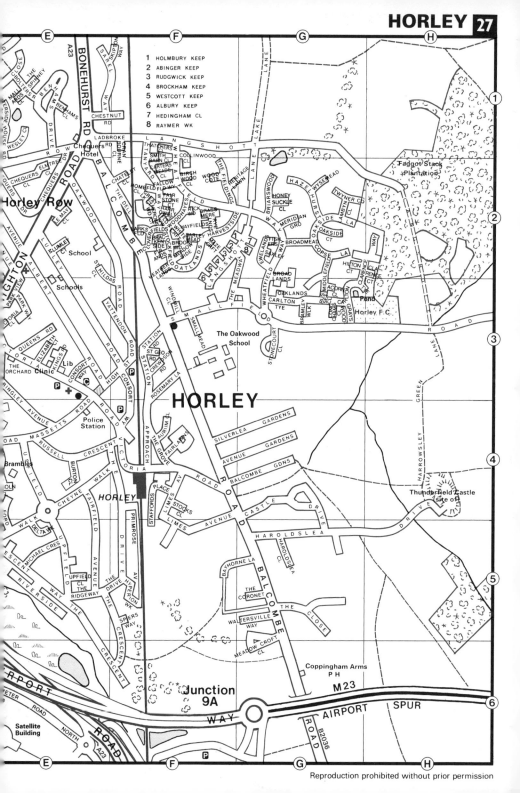

1 HOLMBURY KEEP
2 ABINGER KEEP
3 RUDGWICK KEEP
4 BROCKHAM KEEP
5 WESTCOTT KEEP
6 ALBURY KEEP
7 HEDINGHAM CL
8 RAYMER WK

HORLEY

A - Z INDEX TO STREETS
with Postcodes

The Index includes some names for which there is insufficient space on the maps. These names are preceded by an * and are followed by the nearest adjoining thoroughfare.

BANSTEAD AREA

'he Waplings. KT20 14 C2
'he Warren. KT20 13 E6
'hornfield Rd. SM7 11 F5
'hurnham Way. KT20 12 D4
'ower Rd. KT20 12 C6
'rittons. KT20 13 D4
'roy Clo. KT20 12 B3
'udor Clo. SM7 11 E3
'ulyar Clo. KT20 12 C3
'umblewood Rd. SM7 10 D4
Jpland Way. KT18 10 B6
Jpper Dunnymans Mews. SM7 11 E2
Jpper Sawley Wood. SM7 11 E2

'ernon Walk. KT20 12 D3
'icarage Clo. KT20 15 E1

Valkefield Dri. KT18 10 A5
Wallace Fields, Higher Green. KT17 10 A1
Valnut Dri. KT20 15 E1
Valnut Gro. SM7 10 D2
Valton St. KT20 14 B2
Varren Dri. KT20 13 F5
Varren Lodge. KT20 15 E1
Varren Lodge Dri. KT20 15 E1
Varren Mead. SM7 10 C3
Varren Rd. SM7 10 B2
Vaterer Gdns. KT20 10 D6
Vaterfield. KT20 12 C3
Vaterfield Grn. KT20 12 C4
Vaterhouse La. KT20 13 E4
Vatermead. KT20 12 C4
Vatts La. KT20 12 D5
Vatts Mead. KT20 12 D6
Vellesford Clo. SM7 11 E5
Vessels. KT20 12 D4
Vest Dri. KT20 10 C6
Vhitebeam Way. KT20 12 B4
Vhitegate Way. KT20 12 B3
Vhiteoaks. SM7 11 G1
Villow Bank Gdns. KT20 12 C5
Vilmot Way. SM7 11 F2
Vilsons. KT20 12 D5
Vinkworth Pl. SM7 11 F2
Vinkworth Rd. SM7 11 E2
Vithybed Corner. KT20 14 B1
Vonford Clo. KT20 14 B3
Vood La. KT20 11 E5
Voodgavil. SM7 11 E4
Voodland Way. KT20 13 E5
Voodmansterne La. SM7 11 G3
Voodside. KT20 15 F6

ew Tree Bottom Rd. KT17 10 A4
ewlands Clo. SM7 11 G3

EPSOM & ASHTEAD AREA

delphi Rd. KT19 9 F2
gates La. KT21 6 A3
lbert Rd. KT21 6 C4
lbert Rd. KT17 9 G3
lbert Villas. KT17 9 H4
lexander Godley Clo. KT21 6 D4
lexandra Rd. KT17 9 G2
lmond Rd. KT19 9 F1
nderson Clo. KT19 8 D2
ndrews Clo. KT17 9 G3
pril Clo. KT21 6 C3
quila Clo. KT22 6 B6
sh Mews. KT17 9 G3
shdown Rd. KT17 9 H3
shley Av. KT18 9 F3
shley Ct. KT18 9 F3
shley Rd. KT18 9 F3
shtead Common. KT21 6 A2
shtead Woods Rd. KT21 6 A1
ston Way. KT18 9 H5
venue Rd. KT18 9 F4
xwood. KT18 9 E5

agot Clo. KT21 6 D1
alquhain Clo. KT21 6 B2
arn Clo. KT18 9 E5
arnett Wood La. KT21 6 A3
arons Hurst. KT18 9 E6
Beaconsfield Pl. KT17 9 G2
Beaconsfield Rd. KT18 7 G4
Beauclare Clo. KT22 6 B6
Beech Croft. KT21 6 C4
Beech Rd. KT18 9 H5
Beech Walk. KT17 9 H1
Beechway. KT17 9 H5
Berkeley Ct. KT21 6 C3
Berkeley Pl. KT18 9 F5
Berry Meade. KT21 6 C2
Berry Walk. KT21 6 C4
Birches Clo. KT18 9 G4
Blacksmiths Clo. KT21 6 C4
Blades Clo. KT22 6 A5
Blenheim Rd. KT19 9 F1
Bourne Gro. KT21 6 A4
Bowyers Clo. KT21 6 C3
Bracken Path. KT18 8 D3
Bramble Walk. KT18 8 D3
Bramley Way. KT21 6 C2
Bridge Rd. KT17 9 H2
Bridle End. KT17 9 H3
Bridle Rd. KT17 9 H3
Broad Mead. KT21 6 C3
Broadhurst. KT21 6 B1
Brookers Clo. KT21 6 A3
Bucknills Clo. KT18 9 E4
Burgh Heath Rd. KT17 9 G4
Burghfield. KT17 9 H5
Burnet Gro. KT19 9 E3
Burnside. KT21 6 C3

Caithness Dri. KT18 9 F4
Carters Rd. KT17 9 H5
Castle Rd. KT18 8 D4
Castle View. KT18 8 D4
Cedar Clo. KT17 9 H4
Cedar Hill. KT18 9 E5
Chaffers Mead. KT21 6 C2
Chalk La. KT21 6 D4
Chalk La. KT18 9 F5
Chalk Paddock. KT18 9 F5
Chalk Pit Road. KT18 7 F4
Chantrey Clo. KT21 6 A5
Chantry Hurst. KT18 9 F5
Chartwell Pl. KT18 9 G4
Chase End. KT19 9 F2
Chase Rd. KT19 9 F2
Chelwood Clo. KT17 9 H2
Cherry Tree La. KT19 8 C2
Chestnut Pl. KT17 9 H1
Chestnut Pl. KT21 6 B5
Cherry Orchard. KT21 7 E3
Christ Church Gdns. KT19 8 D1
Christ Church Mount. KT19 8 D2
Christ Church Pl. KT19 8 D1
Christ Church Rd. KT19 8 A2
Church Rd. KT21 6 B3
Church Rd. KT17 9 G3
Church Side. KT18 8 D3
Church St. KT17 9 G3
Chuters Gro. KT17 9 G1
Clayton Pl. KT17 9 G2
Cleeve Ct. KT17 9 G2
College Av. KT17 9 H4
College Rd. KT17 9 G3
Common Corner. KT18 8 D4
Common Side. KT18 8 C4
Conifer Pk. KT17 9 G1
Copse Edge Av. KT17 9 H3
Court La. KT19 9 E2
Craddocks Av. KT21 6 B2
Crampshaw La. KT21 6 C4
Cray Av. KT21 6 C2
Crispin Clo. KT21 6 C3
Crofton. KT21 6 C3
Culverhay. KT21 6 B1

Darcy Pl. KT21 6 C2
Darcy Rd. KT21 6 C2
Delaporte Clo. KT17 9 G2
Delderfield. KT22 6 B6
Dene Rd. KT21 6 C4
Denham Rd. KT17 9 H2
Depot Rd. KT17 9 G3
Derby Stables Rd. KT18 7 H2
Devitt Clo. KT21 6 D2
Digdens Rise. KT18 9 E5
Dirdene Clo. KT17 9 G2
Dirdene Gdns. KT17 9 G2
Dirdene Gro. KT17 9 G2
Dorking Rd. KT18 9 E4
Dorling Dri. KT17 9 H2
Down House Rd. KT18 7 H3
Downs Av. KT18 9 G4
Downs Hill Rd. KT18 9 G4
Downs Rd. KT18 7 F5
Downs Rd, Epsom. KT18 9 G4
Downs Way. KT18 9 G5
Downside. KT18 9 G3
Druids Clo. KT21 6 C5
Drummond Gdns. KT19 8 D1
Dudley Gro. KT18 9 E4

East St. KT19 9 F2
Eastdean Av. KT18 8 D3
Eastway. KT19 9 F1
Ebbas Way. KT18 8 D4
Ebbisham Rd. KT18 8 D4
Elm Gro. KT18 9 E4
Elmslie Clo. KT18 9 E4
Elmwood Clo. KT21 6 B2
Elmwood Ct. KT21 6 B2
Epsom Rd. KT21 6 B2
Epsom Rd. KT17 9 G1
Ermyn Clo. KT22 6 B6
Ermyn Way. KT22 6 A6
Ethel Bailey Clo. KT19 8 C2

Fairbriar Ct. KT18 9 F3
Fairview Rd. KT17 9 G1
Farm La. KT21 7 E2
Farriers Clo. KT17 9 G1
Farriers Rd. KT17 9 G1
Felstead Rd. KT19 9 F1
Forest Cres. KT21 6 D1
Forest Way. KT21 6 D2
Freshmount Gdns. KT18 8 D1

Gayton Clo. KT21 6 C4
Gaywood Rd. KT21 6 C4
Gladstone Rd. KT21 6 A4
Glebe Rd. KT21 6 A3
Gosfield Rd. KT19 9 F2
Grange Clo. KT22 6 A5
Grange Mount. KT22 6 A5
Grange Rd. KT22 6 A5
Grays La. KT21 6 C4
Green La. KT22 6 A6
Green La. KT21 6 A3
Greenway. KT18 8 C4
Greville Clo. KT21 6 B4
Greville Park Av. KT21 6 B3
Greville Park Rd. KT21 6 B3
Grosvenor Rd. KT18 7 G4
Grove Av. KT17 9 G3
Grove Rd. KT21 6 C4
Grove Rd. KT17 9 G3

Hambledon Hill. KT18 9 E5
Hambledon Vale. KT18 9 E6
Hamilton Clo. KT19 9 E2
Hampton Gro. KT17 9 H1
Harding Rd. KT18 7 G4
Harriotts Clo. KT21 6 A5
Harriotts La. KT21 6 A4
Hatfield Rd. KT21 6 C4
Hatherwood. KT22 6 B6
Hawthorne Pl. KT17 9 G2
Hazon Way. KT19 9 E2
Headley Rd. KT18 7 E3
Heathcote Rd. KT1 9 F3
Hereford Clo. KT18 9 F3
Hessle Gro. KT17 9 H1
High St. KT19 9 F3
Highfields. KT21 6 A4
Highridge Clo. KT18 9 G4
Hillcrest Clo. KT18 9 H5
Hillside Rd. KT21 6 C2
Hook Rd. KT19 9 F1
Hookfield. KT19 9 E3
Horsley Clo. KT19 9 F2
Horton Gdns. KT19 9 E1
Horton Hill. KT19 9 E1
Horton La. KT19 8 C1
Howard Clo. KT21 6 C4
Hunters Clo. KT19 9 E3
Hurst Rd. KT19 9 F1
Hylands Clo. KT18 9 E5
Hylands Mews. KT18 9 E4
Hylands Rd. KT18 9 E5

INDUSTRIAL ESTATES:
Longmead Business Centre. KT19 9 F1
Nonsuch Ind Est. KT17 9 G1

Jackson Clo. KT18 9 F4

Kendor Av. KT19 9 E1
Kiln La. KT17 9 G1
King Shades Wk. KT18 9 F3
Kingsdown Rd. KT17 9 H3
Laburnum Rd. KT18 9 F3
Ladbroke Rd. KT18 9 F4
Lane End. KT18 8 D4
Langlands Rise. KT19 9 E3
Langley Clo. KT18 7 G4
Langley Vale Rd. KT18 7 F5
Langton Av. KT17 9 H1
Leatherhead By-Pass. KT22 6 A6
Leatherhead Rd. KT22 6 A6
Leighton Way. KT18 9 F4
Leith Rd. KT17 9 G2
Lewins Clo. KT18 8 D4
Linden Pit Path. KT22 6 A5
Linden Pl. KT17 9 G2
Lindsay Clo. KT19 9 E3
Links Clo. KT21 6 A2
Links Pl. KT21 6 A2
Links Rd. KT21 6 A2
Links Rd. KT17 9 H3
Lintons La. KT17 9 G2
Little Orchards. KT18 9 G3
Longdown Rd. KT17 9 H3
Longmead Rd. KT19 9 F1
Loop Rd. KT18 9 E5
Loraine Gdns. KT21 6 B2
Lower Court Rd. KT19 9 E1
Lower Hill Rd. KT19 8 D2
Lynwood Av. KT17 9 H4
Lynwood Rd. KT17 9 H4

Madans Walk. KT18 9 F4
Maidenshaw Rd. KT19 9 F2
Malvern Ct. KT18 9 F4
Mannamead. KT18 7 H5
Mannamead Clo. KT18 7 G5
Manor Green Rd. KT19 9 E1
Manor House Ct. KT18 9 E3
Maple Rd. KT21 6 B4
Marneys Clo. KT18 8 C5
Marshalls Clo. KT18 9 E3
Mathias Clo. KT18 9 E3
Mead End. KT21 6 C2
Meadow Ct. KT18 9 E3
Meadow Rd. KT21 6 B2
Meadway. KT19 9 E2
Middle Clo. KT17 9 G2
Middle La. KT17 9 G2
Miena Way. KT21 6 A2
Milburn Walk. KT18 9 G5
Miles Rd. KT19 9 F2
Mill Rd. KT17 9 G2
Millers Copse. KT18 7 G4
Milton Gdns. KT17 9 G3
Moat Ct. KT21 6 B3
Mole Valley Pl. KT21 6 B5
Mospey Cres. KT17 9 H4
Mynns Clo. KT18 8 D4

Newton Wood Rd. KT21 6 C1
Norman Av. KT17 9 H2
North Fields. KT21 6 B4

Oak Glade. KT19 8 C2
Oak Hill. KT18 9 F5
Oak Leaf Clo. KT19 9 E2
Oak Way. KT21 6 D2
Oaken Coppice. KT21 6 D4
Oakfield Rd. KT21 6 B3
Oakhill Rd. KT21 6 A3
Oakmead Grn. KT18 9 E5
Old Barn Rd. KT18 7 F2
Old Ct. KT21 6 B5
Oldfield Gdns. KT21 6 A4
Orchard Dri. KT21 6 A5
Orchard Gdns. KT18 9 E4
Ottways Av. KT21 6 B5
Ottways La. KT21 6 A5
Overdale. KT21 6 B1

Paddocks Clo. KT21 6 B4
Paddocks Way. KT21 6 B4
Park Hill Rd. KT17 9 H1
Park La. KT21 6 C3
Park Rd. KT21 6 B4
Park Walk. KT21 6 C4
Parkers Clo. KT21 6 C4
Parkers Hill. KT21 6 C4
Parkers La. KT21 6 C4
Parklawn Av. KT18 8 D3
Pauls Pl. KT21 7 E4
Pebble La. KT18 7 E6
Pepys Clo. KT21 6 D2
Petters Rd. KT21 6 C2
Pikes Hill. KT17 9 G2
Pine Hill. KT18 9 F5
Pitt Pl. KT17 9 G3
Pitt Rd. KT17 9 G3
Pleasure Pit Rd. KT21 7 E3
Pond Pl. KT21 6 B2
Portland Pl. KT17 9 G1
Pound Ct. KT21 6 C3
Pound La. KT17 9 F1
Preston Gro. KT21 6 A2
Prospect Pl. KT17 9 G2
Providence Pl. KT17 9 G2
Purcells Clo. KT21 6 C4

Quennell Clo. KT21 6 C4

Ralliwood Rd. KT21 6 D4
Randolph Rd. KT17 9 G4
Read Rd. KT21 6 A3
Rectory Clo. KT21 6 C4
Rectory La. KT21 6 C4
Richbell Clo. KT21 6 A3
Richmond Clo. KT18 9 G3
Ridgeway. KT19 9 E2
Roebuck Clo. KT21 6 B5
Rookery Hill. KT21 6 D3
Rosebank. KT18 9 E3
Rosebery Av. KT17 9 G4
Rosebery Rd. KT18 7 G4
*Rosedale, Oakhill Rd. KT21 6 A3
Ruthen Clo. KT18 8 D4
Rutland Clo. KT21 6 B2

Saddlers Way. KT18 7 G4
St Edith Clo. KT18 9 E4
St Elizabeth Dri. KT18 9 E4
St Georges Gdns. KT17 9 H4
St James Clo. KT18 9 F3
St Johns Av. KT17 9 H2
St Margarets Dri. KT18 9 E4
St Martins Av. KT18 9 G4
St Martins Clo. KT17 9 G3
St Stephens Av. KT21 6 B2
St Theresa Clo. KT18 9 E4
Sharon Clo. KT19 9 E2
Shaw Clo. KT17 9 H1
Sheep Walk. KT18 7 G6
Shephards Walk. KT18 7 E6
Sheraton Dri. KT19 9 E2
Shires Clo. KT21 6 A4
Skinners La. KT21 6 A3
South St. KT18 9 F3
Southview Rd. KT21 6 B4
Spa Dri. KT18 8 C4
Spencer Clo. KT18 7 H5
Spread Eagle Wk. KT18 9 F3
Squirrels Way. KT18 9 F4
Stag Leys. KT21 6 B6
Stamford Green Rd. KT18 8 D3
Station App. KT19 9 F3
Station Way. KT19 9 F3
Stevens Clo. KT17 9 G2
Stones Rd. KT17 9 G1
Stonny Croft. KT21 6 C2
Strand Clo. KT18 7 G4
Summerfield. KT21 6 A4
Sunnybank. KT18 9 E6
Sweet Briar La. KT18 9 F4

Taleworth Pk. KT21 6 B5
Taleworth Rd. KT21 6 A5
Taylor Rd. KT21 6 A3
Temple Rd. KT19 9 F2
The Byways. KT21 6 A3
The Cedars. KT22 6 B6
The Chase. KT21 6 A3
The Crescent. KT18 8 C4
The Green. KT17 9 H1
The Greenway. KT18 8 C4
The Grove. KT17 9 G3
The Hayes. KT18 7 G5
The Hilders. KT21 7 E2
The Marld. KT21 6 C3
The Mead. KT21 6 B4
The Murreys. KT21 6 A3
The Oaks. KT18 9 G4
The Parade. KT18 9 F3
The Pings. KT21 7 E3
The Pointers. KT21 6 B6
The Priors. KT21 6 A5
The Renmans. KT21 6 C1
The Ridge. KT18 7 F3
The Ridings. KT21 6 A2
The Ridings. KT18 9 G4
The Spinney. KT18 9 F3
The Street. KT21 6 C4
The Topiary. KT21 6 B6
The Warren. KT21 6 C5
Timberhill. KT21 6 B4
Tintagel Clo. KT17 9 G3

Treadwell Rd. KT18 9 G5
Treemount Ct. KT17 9 G3

Uplands. KT21 6 B5
Upper Court Rd. KT19 9 E1
Upper High St. KT17 9 G2

Vancouver Clo. KT19 9 E1
Victoria Pl. KT17 9 G2
Virginia Clo. KT21 6 B4

Wallace Fields. KT17 9 H2
Walnut Clo. KT18 9 G5
Walters Mead. KT21 6 B2
Walton Rd. KT18 7 F6
Warren Hill. KT18 9 F6
Warwick Gdns. KT21 6 A3
Waterloo Rd. KT19 9 F2
Well Way. KT18 8 C4
Wells Rd. KT18 8 C4
West Farm Av. KT21 6 A4
West Farm Clo. KT21 6 A4
West Farm Dri. KT21 6 A4
West Field. KT21 6 C3
West Hill. KT19 9 E3
West Hill Av. KT19 9 E2
West Park Rd. KT19 8 C2
West St. KT18 9 E3
Westgate Clo. KT18 9 F4
Westlands Ct. KT18 9 E4
Weston Rd. KT17 9 G1
Wheelers La. KT18 8 D3
White Horse Dri. KT18 9 E4
Whitmores Clo. KT18 9 E5
Willis Clo. KT18 8 D3
Willows Path. KT18 8 D4
Wilmerhatch La. KT18 7 E3
Wimborne Av. KT17 9 G3
Windmill Av. KT17 9 H1
Windmill Clo. KT17 9 H2
Windmill End. KT17 9 H2
Windmill La. KT17 9 H1
Wishford Ct. KT21 6 C3
Woodcote Clo. KT18 9 F4
Woodcote End. KT18 9 F5
Woodcote Green Rd. KT18 9 E5
Woodcote Hurst. KT18 9 E6
Woodcote Hurst Ct. KT18 9 F5
*Woodcote Mews, Worple Rd. KT18 9 F4
Woodcote Pk Rd. KT18 9 E5
Woodcote Rd. KT18 9 F4
Woodcote Side. KT18 7 E1
Woodfield. KT21 6 B2
Woodfield Clo. KT21 6 A2
Woodfield La. KT21 6 B2
Woodfield Rd. KT21 6 B2
Woodlands. KT21 6 C3
Woodlands Rd. KT18 8 C5
Woodlands Way. KT18 8 C6
Woodstock Ct. KT18 9 F2
Wootton Clo. KT18 9 G5
Worlds End. KT18 7 G1
Worple Rd. KT18 9 F4
Wyeths Clo. KT17 9 G3
Wyeths Rd. KT17 9 G3

Yeomanry Clo. KT17 9 G2
Yew Tree Gdns. KT18 9 E5

HORLEY

Abinger Keep. RH6 27 F2
Acorn Clo. RH6 27 G3
Airport Way. RH6 27 E6
Albert Rd. RH6 27 E2
Albury Keep. RH6 27 F2
Arne Gro. RH6 26 C1
Ashleigh Clo. RH6 26 D3
Aurum Clo. RH6 27 F4
Avenue Gdns. RH6 27 F4
Avondale Clo. RH6 26 D1

Baden Gro. RH6 26 C2
Bakehouse Rd. RH6 27 E1
Balcombe Gdns. RH6 27 F4
Balcombe Rd. RH6 27 E2
Barley Mead. RH6 27 F2
Bay Clo. RH6 26 C2
Bayfield Rd. RH6 26 C2
Bayhorne La. RH6 27 F5
Benhams Clo. RH6 27 E1
Benhams Dri. RH6 27 E1
Birchwood Clo. RH6 27 F2

Blundell Av. RH6 26 D2
Bolters Rd. RH6 27 E1
Bolters Rd Sth. RH6 26 D1
Bonehurst Rd. RH6 27 E1
Brackenside. RH6 27 F2
Bramley Walk. RH6 27 G3
Bremner Av. RH6 26 D2
Briars Wood. RH6 27 G2
Brighton Rd. RH6 26 D4
Broadlands. RH6 27 G2
Broadmead. RH6 27 G2
Brockham Keep. RH6 27 F2
Brookwood. RH6 27 F2
Bullfinch Clo. RH6 26 C2
Burton Clo. RH6 27 E4

Cargo Forecourt Rd. RH6 26 B6
Cargo Rd. RH6 26 B6
Carlton Tye. RH6 27 G3
Carters Meade Clo. RH6 27 F2
Castle Dri. RH6 27 G4
Chaffinch Way. RH6 26 C2
Chantry Clo. RH6 26 D2
Charlesfield Rd. RH6 26 D2
Charm Clo. RH6 26 C1
Chatelet Clo. RH6 26 C1
Chequers Clo. RH6 27 E2
Chequers Dri. RH6 27 E2
Chesters. RH6 26 C1
Chestnut Rd. RH6 27 E1
Cheyne Walk. RH6 26 D5
Church Rd. RH6 26 D4
Church Walk. RH6 26 D4
Churchview Clo. RH6 26 D4
Clarence Rd. RH6 27 H2
Clarence Way. RH6 27 G3
Cloverfields. RH6 27 F2
Collingwood Clo. RH6 27 F1
Consort Way. RH6 27 E3
Copse La. RH6 27 F2
Court Lodge Rd. RH6 26 C2
Cranbourne Clo. RH6 27 F1
Crescent Way. RH6 27 E5
Crewdson Rd. RH6 27 F3
Crossway. RH6 27 F2
Crutchfield La. RH6 26 A1

Darenth Way. RH6 26 D1
Deepfields. RH6 26 D1
Delta Walk. RH6 27 E5
Dene Clo. RH6 26 C1
Downe Clo. RH6 26 C1
Drake Rd. RH6 26 C3

Elizabeth Ct. RH6 27 E3
Elmtree Clo. RH6 27 E2
Emlyn Rd. RH6 26 C2
Ewelands. RH6 27 G2

Fairfield Av. RH6 27 E4
Fairlawns. RH6 27 F4
Fairstone Ct. RH6 27 F2
Fallowfield Way. RH6 27 F2
Ferndown. RH6 27 E1
Fieldview. RH6 27 F2
Firlands. RH6 27 F2
Fishers. RH6 27 G2
Furlong Way. RH6 26 D6

Gatwick Way. RH6 26 D6
Goldcrest Clo. RH6 26 C2
Gower Rd. RH6 26 C3
Granary Clo. RH6 27 E1
Grassmere. RH6 27 F2
Grays Wood. RH6 27 G3
Greatlake Ct. RH6 27 F2
Greenfields Clo. RH6 26 C1
Greenfields Rd. RH6 26 D1
Grendon Clo. RH6 27 E3
Grove Rd. RH6 26 D2

Hardy Clo. RH6 26 C3
Haroldslea Clo. RH6 27 G5
Haroldslea Dri. RH6 27 G5
Harrowsley Ct. RH6 27 F2
Harrowsley Green La. RH6 27 H4
Harvestside. RH6 27 F2
Hatchgate. RH6 26 D4
Hayfields. RH6 27 G2
Hazelhurst. RH6 27 G2
Heatherlands. RH6 27 F2
Hedingham Clo. RH6 27 G2
Heritage Lawn. RH6 27 F2
Heronswood Ct. RH6 27 F2
Hevers Av. RH6 26 D2
High St. RH6 27 E3

Hilton Ct. RH6 27 G2
Holmbury Keep. RH6 27 F2
Homefield Clo. RH6 27 F2
Honeysuckle Clo. RH6 27 G2
Hookwood Rd. RH6 26 B4
Horley Rd. RH6 26 A6
Horley Row. RH6 26 D2
Horse Hill. RH6 26 A3
Hurst Rd. RH6 26 C2
Hutchins Farm. RH6 26 D1
Hutchins Way. RH6 26 D1
Hyperion Walk. RH6 27 F5

Kelsey Clo. RH6 26 D3
Kidworth Clo. RH6 26 D1
Kiln La. RH6 26 C2
Kimberley Clo. RH6 26 D3
Kings Rd. RH6 27 E3
Kingsley Clo. RH6 26 D1
Kingsley Rd. RH6 26 D1

Ladbroke Rd. RH6 27 E1
Lake La. RH6 27 G1
Lambyn Clo. RH6 26 D1
Landen Pk. RH6 26 C1
Langshott. RH6 27 F1
Langshott La. RH6 27 F2
Larksfield. RH6 27 F2
Le May Clo. RH6 27 E2
Lechford Rd. RH6 27 E4
Lee St. RH6 26 C2
Limes Av. RH6 27 F4
Lincoln Clo. RH6 26 C2
London Rd. RH6 26 D5
Longbridge Gate. RH6 26 D6
Longbridge Rd. RH6 26 D5
Longbridge Walk. RH6 26 D5
Longchamp Clo. RH6 27 G3
Lumley Ct. RH6 27 E2
Lumley Rd. RH6 27 E2

Malcolm Gdns. RH6 26 B5
Mallards Clo. RH6 27 E1
Manor Clo. RH6 26 D3
Manor Dri. RH6 26 D3
Massetts Rd. RH6 26 D4
Mazecroft. RH6 27 F2
Meadowcroft Clo. RH6 27 G5
Meadowside. RH6 27 F2
Meathgreen Av. RH6 26 D1
Meathgreen La. RH6 26 C1
Meridian Gro. RH6 27 G2
Michael Cres. RH6 27 E5
Middlefield. RH6 27 E3
Mill Clo. RH6 26 C2
Mill La. RH6 26 B3
Mosford Clo. RH6 26 D1

Newlands Clo. RH6 26 D1
Norfolk Clo. RH6 27 E4
North Way. RH6 26 D6
Northgate Rd. RH6 26 D6

Oaklands. RH6 27 G3
Oakside Clo. RH6 27 G2
Oakside La. RH6 27 G2
Oakwood Rd. RH6 27 E2
Oatlands. RH6 27 F2
Oldfield Clo. RH6 26 D5
Oldfield Rd. RH6 26 D4
Orchard Clo. RH6 26 D2

Palmer Clo. RH6 26 C1
Park Lawn Av. RH6 27 E2
Park View. RH6 27 E2
Parkhurst Gro. RH6 26 D2
Parkhurst Rd. RH6 26 C2
Parkway. RH6 27 E3
Parsons Clo. RH6 26 C2
Perimeter Rd Nth. RH6 27 E6
Pine Gdns. RH6 27 E4
Povey Cross Rd. RH6 26 C5
Powell Clo. RH6 26 C2
Poynes Rd. RH6 26 C1
Primrose Av. RH6 26 C2
Priory Clo. RH6 26 D2

Queens Rd. RH6 27 E3

Racecourse Way. RH6 26 D6
Ramsey Rd. RH6 26 D3
Raymer Walk. RH6 27 G2
Reigate Rd. RH6 26 A1
Rickwood. RH6 27 F2
Ringley Av. RH6 27 E3
Riverside. RH6 27 E5
Roffey Clo. RH6 26 D3
Rosemary Ct. RH6 26 C2

Rosemary La. RH6 27 F3
Rudgwick Keep. RH6 27 F2
Russells Cres. RH6 27 E4
Russet Rd. RH6 27 G3
Rutherwick Clo. RH6 26 D3
Ryelands. RH6 27 F2

St Georges Rd. RH6 27 F3
St Hildas Clo. RH6 27 E2
Sangers Dri. RH6 26 D3
Sarel Way. RH6 27 E1
Saxley. RH6 27 G2
Silverlea Gdns. RH6 27 F4
Skipton Way. RH6 27 E1
Smallfield Rd. RH6 27 F3
Smallmead. RH6 27 F3
Smithbarn Clo. RH6 27 F1
South Parade. RH6 26 D2
Southlands Av. RH6 26 D2
Spiers Way. RH6 27 F5
Staffords Pl. RH6 27 F5
Station App. RH6 27 F3
Station Rd. RH6 27 F3
Stockfield. RH6 27 F2
Stocks Clo. RH6 27 F4
Stonecourt Clo. RH6 27 G3
Suffolk Clo. RH6 27 E4

Tanyard Way. RH6 27 F1
Tarham Clo. RH6 26 C1
Thatchers Clo. RH6 27 F1
The Avenue. RH6 26 D4
The Close. RH6 27 G5
The Coronet. RH6 27 G5
The Crescent. RH6 27 E5
The Dell. RH6 27 F2
The Drive. RH6 27 E4
The Fieldings. RH6 27 F2
The Glebe. RH6 26 D3
The Grove. RH6 27 F3
The Meadway. RH6 27 F3
The Ridgeway. RH6 27 E5
The Spinney. RH6 27 E1
Thornton Clo. RH6 26 D3
Thornton Pl. RH6 26 D3
Todds Clo. RH6 26 C1
Tower Clo. RH6 26 C1
Twyner Clo. RH6 27 G2

Upfield. RH6 27 E4
Upfield Clo. RH6 27 E5

Vicarage La. RH6 26 D2
Victoria Clo. RH6 27 E3
Victoria Rd. RH6 27 E3

Wartersville Way. RH6 27 G5
Waterside. RH6 27 E1
Wellington Way. RH6 26 D1
Wesley Clo. RH6 27 E1
West Leas. RH6 26 C1
Westcott Keep. RH6 27 F2
Wheatfield Way. RH6 27 F1
Whitecroft. RH6 27 F2
Whithey Mdws. RH6 26 B5
Whitmore Way. RH6 26 C2
Wickham Clo. RH6 26 D2
Willow Brean. RH6 26 C1
Windmill Clo. RH6 26 C1
Wither Dale. RH6 26 C1
Withey Brook. RH6 26 B5
Wolverton Clo. RH6 26 D5
Wolverton Gdns. RH6 26 D4
Woodcote. RH6 27 F2
Woodhayes. RH6 27 F2
Woodroyd Av. RH6 26 D4
Woodroyd Clo. RH6 26 D5
Wysemead. RH6 27 G2

Yattendon Rd. RH6 27 F3
Yew Tree Clo. RH6 26 D1

LEATHERHEAD & DORKING AREAS

Abinger Clo. RH5 24 C5
Adlers La. RH5 22 A5
Admirals Rd. KT23 3 F3
Agates La. KT21 5 H1
Albany Park Rd. KT22 5 E1
Allen Rd. KT23 3 D3
Amey Dri. KT23 3 E2
Ansell Rd. RH4 23 B3
Aperdele Rd. KT22 4 C2
Arbour Clo. KT22 4 D5

*Archway Mews, Meadowbrook Rd. RH4 23 A
Arundel Rd. RH4 23 A
Ashcombe Rd. RH4 23 A
Ashdale. KT23 3 E
Ashley Clo. KT23 3 B
Ashley Rd. RH4 24 B
Ashwood Pk. KT23 3 E
Atwood. KT23 3 A

Back Alley. RH4 23 B
Badingham Dri. KT23 4 C
Bailey Rd. RH4 24 B
Barclay Clo. KT22 4 A
Barley Mow Ct. RH3 25 C
Barn Meadow La. KT23 3 B
Barnett Clo. KT22 5 F
Barnett Wood La. KT22 5 F
Barrett Rd. KT22 3 F
Barrington Rd. RH4 23 A
Bay Tree Av. KT22 5 F
Beales Rd. KT23 3 D
Beattie Clo. KT23 3 B
Beckley Par. KT23 3 E
Beech Clo. RH4 23 A
Beech Holt. KT22 5 G
Beechwood Park. KT22 5 G
Bell La. KT22 4 C
Bell Lane Clo. KT22 4 C
Belmont Rd. KT22 5 E
Bennetts Farm Pl. KT23 3 B
Bentsbrook Clo. RH5 24 B
Bentsbrook Park. RH5 24 B
Bentsbrook Rd. RH5 24 B
Beresford Rd. RH4 23 B
Bickney Way. KT22 4 A
Bilton Centre Pk. KT22 5 E
*Bishops Cottages, Reigate Rd. RH3 25 A
Blackbrook Rd. RH5 24 D
Blackthorne Rd. KT23 3 E
Blades Clo. KT21 5 H
Blind La. RH3 25 C
Boleyn Walk. KT22 5 E
Bookham Gro. KT23 3 D
Bourne Gro. KT21 5 H
Boxhill Way. RH3 25 B
Bracken Clo. KT23 3 B
Bradley La. RH5 22 A
Brewhouse Rd. RH3 25 B
Bridge St. KT22 5 E
Brockham Grn. RH3 25 B
Brockham La. RH3 25 A
Broderick Gro. KT23 3 C
Brook Clo. RH4 23 C
Brook Way. KT22 4 B
Broomfield Park. RH4 24 B
Browning Rd. KT22 3 F
Brympton Clo. RH4 23 A
Buffers La. KT22 5 F
Bull Hill. KT22 5 F
Burney Clo. KT22 3 E
Burney Rd. RH5 22 A
Burnhams Rd. KT23 3 A
Burrows Clo. KT23 3 E
Bushbury La. RH3 25 A
Bushey Shaw. KT21 4 D
Bushy Rd. KT22 4 A
Byron Pl. KT22 5 F
Byttom Hill. RH5 22 C

Caen Wood Rd. KT21 4 D
Calvert Cres. RH4 23 B
Calvert Rd. RH4 23 B
Camilla Clo. KT23 3 C
Camilla Dri. RH5 22 A
Candy Croft. KT23 3 C
Cannon Gro. KT22 4 C
Cannon Way. KT22 4 C
Cannonside. KT22 4 C
Cedar Cr. RH4 23 B
Cedar Dri. KT22 4 D
Chalkpit La. RH3 25 B
Chalkpit La. RH4 23 A
Chalkpit Ter. RH4 23 A
Challenge Ct. KT22 5 F
Chantrey Clo. KT21 5 H
Chapel La. RH4 23 A
Chapel La. RH4 24 A
Chapel La. RH5 22 A
Chardhurst Clo. RH5 24 C
Charlwood Clo. KT23 3 B
Chart Clo. RH5 23 6
Chart Downs. RH5 24 C
Chart La. RH4 23 B
Chart La Sth. RH5 23 C
Chequers Yd. RH4 23 A

Cherkley Hill. KT22 22 C2
Chester Clo. RH4 23 C2
Chichester Clo. RH4 23 B2
Chichester Rd. RH4 23 B1
Childs Hall Clo. KT23 3 B3
Childs Hall Dri. KT23 3 B2
Childs Hall Rd. KT23 3 B2
Chilmans Dri. KT23 3 D3
Christie Clo. KT23 3 B3
Christy La. KT23 3 D3
Church Clo. KT23 3 F1
Church Gdns. RH4 23 B3
Church Rd. KT23 3 B1
Church Rd. KT22 5 F4
Church St. RH3 25 D3
Church St. RH4 23 A4
Church St. KT22 5 F4
Church Walk. KT22 5 F4
Churchill Clo. KT22 4 C5
Clandon Mews. RH4 24 A4
Clare Cres. KT22 4 C2
Clare Wood. KT22 4 C2
Claremont Clo. RH4 23 A5
Claygate Rd. RH4 23 B6
Cleardene RH4 23 B4
Cleeve Rd. KT22 5 E2
Cliftonville. RH4 23 B5
Clinton Rd. KT22 5 G5
Coach Rd. RH3 25 A3
Cobham Rd. KT22 4 A3
Cock La. KT22 4 C2
Coldharbour La. RH4 23 A6
Commonside. KT23 3 C1
Copperfield Ct. KT22 5 F3
Copperfields. KT22 4 A4
Copthorne Rd. KT23 5 F2
Corfe Clo. KT21 4 D1
Crabtree Clo. KT23 3 E3
Crabtree Dri. KT22 22 C1
Crabtree La. KT23 3 E3
Crabtree La. RH5 22 A4
Cradhurst Clo. RH4 24 A2
Cressel Clo. KT22 5 F2
Cressel Mead. KT22 5 F2
Croft Av. RH4 23 B2
Curtis Gdns. RH4 23 A3
Curtis Rd. RH4 23 A3

Dawnay Rd. KT23 3 D4
Daymerslea Ridge. KT22 5 G3
Dean Walk. KT23 3 D3
Deepdene Av. RH4 23 C4
Deepdene Av. Rd. RH4 23 C2
Deepdene Dri. RH5 23 C3
Deepdene Gdns. RH4 23 C3
Deepdene Park Rd. RH5 23 D3
Deepdene Vale. RH4 23 C3
Deepdene Wood. RH5 23 C4
Dell Clo. KT22 4 C5
Dell Clo. RH5 22 C3
Dene St. RH4 23 B4
Dene St Gdns. RH4 23 B4
Denfield. RH4 23 B5
Diston Rd. KT22 5 E1
Dodds Park. RH3 25 B4
Dorking By-Pass. RH4 23 C6
Dorking Rd, Gt Bookham. KT23 3 D3
Dorking Rd, Leatherhead. KT22 5 F6
Dorking Rd, Mickleham. KT22 22 B1
Dowlans Clo. KT23 3 C4
Dowlans Rd. KT23 3 D4
Downs La. KT22 5 F5
Downs View. RH4 3 D4
Downs View Rd. KT23 3 E4
Downs Way. KT22 3 E3
Downsview Gdns. RH4 23 B5
Drayton Clo. KT22 4 C6
Dukes Ride. RH4 23 B5
Durleston Pk Dri. KT23 3 E2

East St. KT23 3 D3
Eastwick Dri. KT23 3 D1
Eastwick Park Av. KT23 3 D2
Eastwick Rd. KT22 3 D2
Ebisham Clo. RH4 23 A4
Eccles Hill. RH5 24 B5
Elmside Rd. KT23 3 B1
Elgeley. RH3 3 A1
Elder Way. RH5 24 C5
Elm Clo. KT22 5 F4
Elm Dri. KT22 5 F4
Elm Rd. KT22 5 F4
Elm Villas, Old Reigate Rd. RH3 25 B2

Elmer Cotts. KT22 5 E5
Elmer Mews. KT22 5 E4
Elmhurst Dri. RH4 23 B6
Elmswood. KT23 3 B1
Emerton Rd. KT22 4 B3
Emlyn La. KT22 5 E4
Ensom Rd. KT22 5 H4
Ermyn Way. KT21 5 H3

Fairfield Clo. KT23 3 D3
Fairfield Dri. RH4 23 B2
Fairfield Rd. KT22 5 F3
Fairfield Walk. KT22 5 F3
Fairholme Cres. KT21 4 D1
Fairlawn. KT23 3 B2
Fairs Rd. KT22 5 E1
Falcon Wood. KT22 5 E2
Falkland Gdns. RH4 23 A5
Falkland Rd. RH4 23 A5
Farm Clo. KT22 4 C6
Fernlea. KT23 3 D1
Fetcham Common La. KT22 4 A3
Fetcham Park Dri. KT22 4 D5
Fife Way. KT23 3 C2
Fiona Clo. KT23 3 C1
Fir Tree Clo. KT22 5 H5
Fir Tree Rd. KT22 5 G5
Firs Clo. RH4 23 A6
Flint Clo. KT23 3 E3
Flint Hill. RH4 23 B6
Flint Hill Clo. RH4 24 B4
Floral Ct. KT21 4 D1
Fortyfoot Rd. KT22 5 G3
Fox Covert. KT22 3 F2
Fox La. KT23 3 B2
Fraser Gdns. RH4 23 A3
Friars Orchard. KT22 4 B3
Furlong Rd. RH4 24 A2

Garden Clo. KT22 5 G6
Gardeners Walk. KT23 3 D4
Garendon Clo. KT22 22 C1
Garlands Rd. KT22 5 G3
Gatesden Rd. KT22 4 B5
Gaveston Rd. KT22 5 E2
Gilmais. KT23 3 E3
Gimcrack Hill. KT22 5 F4
Givons Gro. KT22 22 C1
Glebe Clo. KT23 3 C3
Glebe Rd. RH4 24 D1
Glenfield Clo. RH3 25 B5
Glenfield Rd. RH3 25 B5
Glenheadon Clo. KT22 5 H5
Glenheadon Rise. KT22 5 H5
Glenwood. RH4 24 B4
Glory Mead. RH4 24 B4
Goldstone Farm Vw. KT23 3 C4
Goodwyns Rd. RH4 24 B4
Grange Clo. KT22 5 H2
Grange Mt. KT22 5 H2
Grange Rd. KT22 5 H2
Gravel Hill. KT22 5 F3
Greathurst End. KT23 3 C1
Green La. KT22 5 H3
Greenacres. KT23 3 C1
Greenway. KT23 3 D1
Greville Ct. KT23 3 D2
Griffin Way. KT23 3 C3
Groveside. KT23 3 C4
Groveside Clo. KT23 3 C4
Guildford Rd. KT23 3 B4
Guildford Rd. KT22 4 C6
Guildford Rd. KT22 24 A3

Hale Pit Rd. KT23 3 E3
Hales Oak. KT23 3 E3
Hampstead La. RH4 23 A5
Hampstead Rd. RH4 23 A5
Hanover Ct. RH4 24 D1
Hardy Clo. RH4 24 B5
Hare Croft. RH4 24 C4
Harecroft. KT23 3 E1
Harriotts Clo. KT21 5 H2
Harriotts La. KT21 5 G1
Harrow Clo. RH4 23 A5
Harrow Rd E. RH4 23 B5
Harrow Rd W. RH4 23 A5
Harrowlands Pk. RH4 23 B5
Hart Gdns. RH4 23 B3
Hart Rd. RH4 23 B3
Hartswood. RH5 24 C4
Hatherwood. KT23 3 C4
Hawks Hill. KT22 5 H3
Hawks Hill. KT22 5 E5
Hawks Hill Clo. KT22 5 E5
Hawks Hill Ct. KT22 5 E5
Hawkwood Dell. KT23 3 C3

Hawkwood Rise. KT23 3 C3
*Hazel Parade, Penrose Rd. KT22 4 A4
Hazel Walk. RH5 24 C4
Hazel Way. KT22 4 A4
Hazelmere Clo. KT22 5 F1
Headley Rd. KT22 5 H4
Heath Hill. RH4 23 B2
Heath Rise. RH4 24 A3
Heathersland Rd. RH4 24 C4
Heymede. KT22 5 G5
High Meadow Clo. RH4 23 B5
High St. RH4 23 B4
High St. KT23 3 D3
High St. KT22 5 F4
Highacre. KT22 23 B6
Highfields. KT22 3 F1
Highfields. KT21 5 H1
Highlands Av. KT22 5 G4
Highlands Clo. KT22 5 G4
Highlands Pk. KT22 5 H5
Highlands Rd. KT22 5 G4
Highwoods. KT22 5 G3
Hill Rise. RH4 23 A2
Hill Road. RH4 24 A4
Hilley Field La. KT22 5 E4
Hillside Clo. RH3 25 A2
Hillside Gdns. RH3 25 A2
Hilltop Clo. KT22 5 G5
Hilltop Rise. KT23 3 E3
Holly Ct. KT22 5 E4
Holmbury Dri. RH5 24 C5
Holmesdale Rd. RH5 24 B5
Home Clo. KT22 4 C3
Homefield Clo. KT23 5 G3
Homelands. KT22 5 G3
Honeysuckle La. RH5 24 C4
Horsham Rd. RH4 23 A5
Horsham Rd. RH5 24 B4
Howard Clo. KT22 5 G5
Howard Rd. RH4 23 A4
Howard Rd. KT23 3 D4
Howard Rd. RH5 24 B5
Hulton Clo. KT22 5 G5
Humphrey Clo. KT22 4 A4
Huntsmans Clo. KT22 3 F2

INDUSTRIAL ESTATES:
Bookham Ind Est. KT23 3 B1
Dorking Business Pk. RH4 23 A3
Haverbury Ind Est. RH4 23 A3
Leatherhead Ind. Est. KT22 5 E3
Mole Business Pk. KT22 5 E3
Regent Park Ind Area. KT22 4 B2
Research Area. KT22 5 G2
Inholms La. RH5 24 B5
Institute Rd. RH4 24 A2

Jubilee Rd. KT23 3 B3
Jubilee Te. RH3 25 B6
Junction Rd. RH4 23 A4

Kelvin Av. KT22 5 E2
Kennel Clo. KT22 3 E1
Kennel La. KT22 4 A4
Keppel Rd. RH4 23 A2
Keswick Rd. KT23 3 E2
Kidborough Down. KT23 3 C4
Kingsbrook. KT22 4 B2
Kingscroft Rd. KT22 5 F2
Kingslea. KT22 5 F2
Kingston Av. KT22 5 F3
Kingston House Gdns. KT22 5 F3
Kingston Rd. KT22 5 F1
Knoll Rd. RH4 23 A6

Ladygate Clo. RH5 23 C3
Ladygate Rd. RH5 23 C4
Lake View. RH5 24 C4
Langalier La. KT23 3 D1
Langalier La. RH4 4 A4
Larkspur Way. RH5 24 B4
Leach Gro. KT22 5 G4
Leatherhead By-Pass. KT22 5 G2
Leatherhead Rd. KT23 3 E3
Leatherhead Rd. KT22 5 H3
Leith View. RH5 24 C5
Leret Way. KT22 5 F3
Leslie Rd. RH4 23 D2
Levett Rd. KT22 5 G2
Lime Tree Clo. KT23 3 C1

Limeway Ter. RH4 23 A2
Lince La. RH4 24 B2
Lincoln Rd. RH4 23 B2
Linden Ct. KT22 5 F3
Linden Gdns. KT22 5 G3
Linden Pit Path. KT22 5 F3
Linden Rd. KT22 5 F3
Links Brow. KT22 4 D5
Links Rd. KT22 4 D1
Links View Av. RH3 25 A2
Little Bookham St. KT23 3 B1
Little Borough. RH3 25 A3
Lodge Clo. KT22 4 B4
Lodge Clo. RH5 24 B5
Lodge Rd. KT22 4 B4
Logmore La. RH4 24 A3
London Rd. RH4 23 B3
London Rd. RH5 22 B6
Long Copse Clo. KT22 3 D1
Long Meadow. KT23 3 B3
Longfield Rd. RH4 24 D2
Longheath Dri. KT23 3 A2
Longshaw. KT22 5 E2
Lonsdale Rd. RH4 23 B3
Lowburys. RH4 24 A4
Lower Rd. KT22 4 C5
Lower Rd. KT23 3 A4
Lower Shott. KT23 3 C3
Lusteds Clo. RH4 24 B4
Lyons Ct. RH4 23 B4

Maddox La. KT23 3 A1
Maddox Pk. KT23 3 A1
Magazine Pl. KT22 5 F4
Magnolia Way. RH4 24 D4
Manor House La. KT23 3 A3
Maplehurst. KT22 4 B5
Market Pl. RH4 23 B3
Marlborough Hill. RH4 23 B4
Marlborough Rd. RH4 23 B4
Marley Rise. KT22 24 A4
Martineau Dri. RH4 23 B6
Masons Paddock. RH4 23 A2
Mayell Clo. KT22 5 G5
Mayfield Grn. KT23 3 C4
Mead Cres. KT22 3 C2
Meadow La. KT22 4 B4
Meadow Way. KT22 4 A5
Meadowbrook Rd. RH4 23 A3
Meadowside. KT23 3 C1
Medefield. KT22 3 F1
Melvin Shaw. KT22 5 G3
Merrylands Rd. KT23 3 B1
Merton Way. KT22 4 C2
Mickleham By-Pass. RH5
Mickleham Dri. KT22 22 C2
Middle Rd. KT22 5 F3
Middle St. RH3 25 B3
Middlemead Clo. KT23 3 C3
Middlemead Rd. KT23 3 B2
Mill Clo. KT23 3 C2
Mill La. RH4 23 B3
Mill La. KT22 5 E4
Millhill La. RH3 25 B2
Milton Av. RH4 24 B2
Milton St. RH4 24 B2
Milton Way. RH4 3 E2
Miltoncourt La. RH4 24 C1
Minchin Clo. KT22 5 E2
Mint Gdns. RH4 23 A3
Mole Rd. KT22 4 C1
Mole Valley Pl. KT21 5 H1
Monks Grn. KT22 4 B3
Moores Rd. RH4 23 B3
Mount Clo. KT22 4 D5
Mount St. RH4 23 A4
Mowbray Gdns. RH4 23 B2
Murrelles Walk. KT23 3 B1
Myrtle Rd. RH4 23 A3

New Rd. RH5 23 C5
New Rd. RH3 25 B4
Newenham Rd. KT23 3 C3
Norbury Way. KT23 3 E3
Norfolk Rd. RH4 23 A4
North Clo. RH4 24 C5
North St, Dorking. RH4 23 A4
North St, Leatherhead. KT22 5 F3
North St, Westcott. RH4 24 A2
Nower Rd. RH4 23 A4
Nutcombe La. RH4 24 D1
Nutcroft Gro. KT22 4 C3
Nutwood Av. RH3 25 B2
Nutwood Clo. RH3 25 B2

Oak Ridge. RH4 24 B4
Oak Rd. KT22 4 B2
Oakbank. KT22 4 B5
Oakdene Clo. RH3 25 C4
Oakdene Clo. KT23 3 E4
Oakdene Rd. RH3 25 B4
Oakdene Rd. KT23 3 B2
Oakhill Clo. KT22 4 D2
Oakhill Rd. KT22 4 D2
Oaklands. KT22 3 F1
Oaklawn Rd. KT22 4 A1
Oaks Clo. KT22 5 F3
Old Kiln La. RH3 25 B2
Old London Rd. RH5 22 C3
Old Reigate Rd. RH3 25 B2
Old Road. RH3 25 D1
Old School La. RH3 25 A6
Old Station App. KT22 5 E3
Orchard Clo, Fetcham. KT22 4 C4
Orchard Clo, Givons Grove. KT22 22 C1
Orchard Dri. KT21 5 H2
Orchard End. KT22 3 E2
Orchard Leigh. KT22 5 G4
Orchard Rd. RH4 23 B5
Orchard Way. RH4 23 B5
Osprey Clo. KT22 4 B4
Oswald Clo. KT22 4 B4
Oswald Rd. KT22 4 B4
Ottways La. KT21 5 H2
Overdale. RH5 23 C3
Oveton Way. KT23 3 D3
Owen Pl. KT22 5 F4
Oxshott Rd. KT22 4 B1

Paper Mews. RH4 23 B3
Park Clo, Fetcham. KT22 4 C6
Park Clo, Leatherhead. KT22 5 F3
Park Clo. RH3 25 B6
Park Copse. RH5 23 D4
Park Grn. KT23 3 C1
Park Pale La. RH3 25 A6
Park Rise. KT22 5 F3
Park Vw. KT23 3 C2
Park Way. KT23 3 C1
Parklands. KT23 3 C1
Parklands. RH5 24 B5
Parkway. RH4 23 A3
Parr Clo. KT22 5 E2
Parris Croft. RH4 24 C4
Parsonage Clo. RH4 24 A3
Parsonage La. RH4 24 A3
Parsonage Sq. RH4 23 A3
Pelham Way. KT23 3 E3
Penrose Rd. KT22 4 A4
Pilgrims Clo. RH5 22 A5
Pilgrims Way. RH5 22 B5
Pine Dean. KT23 3 D2
Pine Walk. KT23 3 D2
Pippbrook Gdns. RH4 23 B3
Pixham La. RH4 23 C1
Pixholme Gro. RH4 23 C2
Pointers Hill. RH4 24 A2
Polesden View. KT23 3 D4
Poplar Av. KT22 5 G4
Poplar Rd. KT22 5 G4
Portland Rd. RH4 23 A3
Post House La. KT23 3 C2
Pound Cres. KT22 4 C3
Powells Clo. RH4 24 B4
Preston Gro. KT21 4 D1
Priors Mead. KT23 3 E2
Priory Clo. RH4 23 A5
Proctor Gdns. KT23 3 D3
*Puddenhole Cottages, Reigate Rd. RH3 25 A1
Punchbowl La. RH5 23 C3

Queen Annes Gdns. KT22 5 F3
Queen Annes Ter. KT22 5 F3

Randalls Cres. KT22 5 E2
Randalls Farm La. KT22 5 F1
Randalls Park Av. KT22 5 E2
Randalls Park Dri. KT22 5 E3
Randalls Rd. KT22 5 E2
Randalls Way. KT22 5 E2
Ranmore Rd. RH4 23 A2
Raymead Clo. KT22 4 D4
Raymead Way. KT22 4 D4
Rectory La. KT22 3 B3
Reigate Rd. RH4 25 A1
Reigate Rd. RH3 23 C3
Reigate Rd. KT22 5 G4
Research Area. KT22 5 E2

Revell Clo. KT22 4 A4
Revell Dri. KT22 4 A4
Richmond Clo. KT22 3 E1
Richmond Way. KT22 3 D1
Ridge Clo. RH3 25 B6
Ridgelands. KT22 3 F1
Ridgeway Clo. RH4 23 A6
Ridgeway Dri. RH4 24 A4
Ridgeway Rd. RH4 23 A6
River La. KT22 4 B3
Riverside. RH4 23 D2
Roger Simmons Clo. KT23 3 C1
Roman Rd. RH4 23 B6
Rookery Clo. RH4 4 C6
Rose Hill. RH4 23 A4
Rosedale. KT21 4 D2
Rothes Rd. RH4 23 B3
Rough Rew. RH4 24 B4
Rowhurst Av. KT22 4 A1
Rushett Dri. RH4 24 B4
Russell Ct. KT22 5 F4
Russet Way. RH5 24 D4
Ryebridge Clo. KT22 4 C1
Ryebrook Rd. KT22 4 B2
Ryelands Ct. KT22 4 C2

St Brelades Clo. RH4 23 A6
St Johns. RH5 24 B5
St Johns Av. KT22 5 F3
St Johns Clo. KT22 5 G2
St Johns Rd. RH4 24 A2
St Johns Rd. KT22 5 G3
St Martins Mews. RH4 23 A4
St Martins Pl. RH4 23 A3
St Marys Clo. KT22 4 C5
St Marys Rd. KT22 5 F4
St Nicholas Av. KT23 3 D2
St Nicholas Hill. KT22 5 G4
St Pauls Rd East. RH4 23 B4
St Pauls Rd West. RH4 23 A5
Salvation Pl. KT22 5 E6
Sandes Pl. KT22 4 C2
Sayers Clo. KT22 3 E1
School La. KT22 4 C4
School La. RH5 22 C3
School La. RH4 24 B2
Shamrock Clo. KT22 4 C3
Sharon Clo. KT23 3 C1
Shellwood Clo. RH5 24 C5
Shere Clo. RH4 24 C5
Sheridans Rd. KT23 3 E3
Sherwood Clo. KT22 4 B5
Shires Clo. KT21 5 H1
Silverdale Clo. RH3 25 B5
Sole Farm Av. KT23 3 B2
Sole Farm Clo. KT23 3 B2
Sole Farm Rd. KT23 3 B2
Solecote. KT23 3 C2
Sondes Place Dri. RH4 24 D1
South Dri. RH5 23 C4
South End. KT23 3 D3
South St. RH4 23 A5
South Ter. RH4 23 B5
South View Rd. KT21 5 H1
Southey Ct. KT23 3 D2
Spital Heath. RH5 23 C3
Spook Hill. RH5 24 B6
Spring Gdns. RH4 23 A3
Spring Gro. KT23 3 D1
Springfield Rd. RH4 24 A2
Squirrels Grn. KT23 3 C1
Station App. RH4 23 B2
Station App. KT22 5 E3
Station Rd. RH5 25 D1
Station Rd. RH4 23 A4
Station Rd. KT23 5 E3
Stone Hill Clo. KT23 3 C2
Stones La. RH4 24 A2
Stubbs Clo. RH4 23 C6
Stubbs Hill. RH4 24 C4
Styles End. KT23 3 D4
Summerfield. KT21 5 H1
Sumner Clo. KT22 3 F2
Sunmead Clo. KT22 5 E4
Swan Ct. KT22 5 F3
Swan Mill Gdns. RH4 23 C2
Swanns Meadow. KT23 3 C3
Swanworth La. RH5 22 B3
Sycamore Clo. KT22 4 D4

Taleworth Pk. KT21 5 H2
Taleworth Rd. KT21 5 H1
Tanners Dean. KT22 5 H4
Tanners Hill. TH3 25 A3
Tanners Meadow. RH3 25 B6
Tate Clo. KT22 5 G5
Teatle Wood Hill. KT22 4 A1

Teazlewood Park. KT22 4 B1
Ten Acres. KT22 3 F2
Ten Acres Clo. KT22 3 F2
The Approach. KT23 3 B1
The Avenue. RH3 25 A4
The Ballands Nth. KT22 4 C4
The Ballands Sth. KT22 4 C5
The Beeches. KT22 4 D6
The Berkeleys. KT22 4 D6
The Blackburn. KT23 3 B2
The Borough. RH3 25 A3
The Burrell. RH4 24 A2
The Chine. RH4 23 B3
The Close. RH3 25 B6
The Copse. KT22 4 A5
The Crescent. KT22 5 F4
The Downs. KT22 22 C1
The Driftway. KT22 5 G5
The Drive. KT22 4 D4
The Fairway. KT22 4 C2
The Garstons. KT23 3 C2
The Glade. KT22 4 A4
The Green. KT22 3 F2
The Hildens. KT22 24 A3
The Knoll. KT22 5 G3
The Limes. KT22 5 G4
The Lorne. KT23 3 C3
The Mount. KT22 4 D5
The Murreys. KT21 5 H1
The Orchard. RH5 24 C5
The Paddock. RH4 24 A2
The Paddocks. KT23 3 D3
The Park. KT23 3 C1
The Pines. RH4 23 B5
The Priors. KT21 5 H1
The Ridge. KT22 3 F1
The Ridgeway. KT22 4 C5
The Smithers. RH3 25 B4
The Spinney. KT23 3 D2
The Street. RH3 25 D2
The Street. KT22 4 B3
The Terrace. RH5 23 C5
The Twitten. RH4 24 B2
The Walled Gdn. RH3 25 D3
The Withies. KT22 5 G2
Thorncroft Dri. KT22 5 F5
Tilehurst La. RH5 23 D5
Timber Clo. KT23 3 E4
Tollgate Rd. RH4 23 B6
Tower Hill. RH4 23 B6
Tower Hill Rd. RH4 23 B6
Townfield Rd. RH4 23 A5
Townshott Clo. KT23 3 C3
Trasher Mead. RH4 23 C6
Treelands. RH5 24 C4
Tregarthen Pl. KT22 5 G3
Tudor Clo. KT23 3 C2
Tudor Walk. KT22 5 E2
Turville Ct. KT23 3 D3
Tweed La. RH3 25 A6
Twelve Acre Clo. KT23 3 B1
Tynedale Rd. RH3 25 B6

Uplands. KT21 5 H2
Upper Fairfield Rd. KT22 5 F3
Upper Rose Hill. RH4 23 B4

Vaughan La. RH4 23 A4
Vicarage La. KT23 3 C3
Vicarage La. KT22 5 F4
Victoria Ter. RH4 23 A4
Vincent Clo. KT23 3 D1
Vincent Dri. RH4 23 A5
Vincent La. RH4 23 A4
Vincent Rd. RH4 23 A4
Vincent Walk. RH4 23 A4

Wallis Mews. KT22 5 E4
Walford Rd. RH4 24 B5
Warren Rd. KT22 4 B5
Warrenne Rd. RH3 25 B4
Water La. KT23 3 A3
Waterfields. RH4 5 F1
Waterway Rd. KT22 5 E4
Wathen Rd. RH4 23 B3
Watson Rd. RH4 24 B2
Waverley Pl. KT22 5 F4
Wellhouse Rd. RH4 25 C5
Wells Clo. KT23 3 E2
West Bank. RH4 23 A5
West Down. KT23 3 D4
West Farm Av. KT21 5 H1
West Farm Clo. KT21 5 G1
West Farm Dri. KT21 5 H1
West St. RH4 23 A4
Westcott Mews. RH4 24 A2
Westcott Rd. RH4 24 C2
Westcott St. RH4 24 A2

Westhumble St. RH5 22 B5
Westlees Clo. RH5 24 C4
Wheelers La. RH3 25 B4
White Way. KT23 3 D3
Wildcroft Dri. RH5 24 C5
Willow Grn. RH5 24 B5
Willow Mead. RH4 23 A3
Willow Vale. KT22 4 A5
Windfield. KT22 5 G3
Windmill Dri. KT22 5 G5
Wonham La. RH3 25 D3
Woodbridge Av. KT22 4 C2
Woodbridge Gr. KT22 4 C2
Woodend. KT22 5 G6
Woodside. KT22 4 A4
Woodvill Rd. KT22 5 F2
Worple Rd. KT22 5 F4

Yarm Ct Rd. KT22 5 G5
Yarm Way. KT22 5 H5
Yew Tree Rd. RH4 23 A2
Young St. KT22 5 E6

Zig Zag Rd. RH5 22 C4

REIGATE & REDHILL AREA

Abbotts Rise. RH1 19 G1
Abinger Dri. RH1 19 F6
Albany Clo. RH2 18 B1
Albert Rd. RH1 17 E4
Albert Rd North. RH2 18 A2
Albert Rd South. RH2 18 A3
Albion Rd. RH2 18 C4
Albury Rd. RH1 17 E4
Alders Rd. RH2 18 C2
Alexander Rd. RH2 18 B6
Allingham Rd. RH2 18 B6
Alma Rd. RH2 18 C2
Alpine Rd. RH1 16 C6
Altdam Farm. RH1 21 G5
Althorne Rd. RH1 19 G5
Ambleside Clo. RH1 21 H3
Anglo Way. RH1 19 H2
Apley Rd. RH2 20 B1
Arbutus Clo. RH1 18 D6
Arbutus Rd. RH1 18 D6
Arden Clo. RH2 20 C2
Ardshiel Dri. RH1 19 F5
Ash Clo. RH1 17 E5
Ash Dri. RH1 19 H5
Ashcombe Rd. RH1 17 E2
Ashdown Clo. RH2 20 C2
Ashdown Rd. RH2 20 C2
Asylum Arch Rd. RH1 21 G1
Atherfield Rd. RH2 20 D1
Avenue Villas. RH1 17 E4

Back La. RH1 16 A4
Bancroft Ct. RH2 18 B4
Bancroft Rd. RH2 18 B4
Barons Way. RH2 20 B2
Battlebridge La. RH1 16 D5
Batts Hill. RH1 19 E2
Baxter Av. RH1 19 F3
Beaufort Clo. RH2 18 A3
Beaufort Rd. RH2 18 A3
Beaumonts. RH1 21 G6
Beech Dri. RH2 19 E3
Beech Rd. RH1 17 E1
Beech Rd. RH2 18 B1
Beehive Way. RH2 20 C2
Bell St. RH2 18 B4
Belmont Rd. RH1 18 D5
Beverley Heights. RH2 18 C1
Birchway. RH1 19 H5
Birkheads Rd. RH2 18 B2
Blackborough Clo. RH2 18 C4
Blackborough Rd. RH2 18 C4
Blackstone Clo. RH1 19 E4
Blackstone Hill. RH1 19 E4
Blackthorn Clo. RH2 18 D6
Blackthorn Rd. RH2 18 C6
Blanford Rd. RH2 18 B6
Bletchingley Clo. RH1 17 E4
Bletchingley Rd. RH1 17 E3
Bolsover Gro. RH1 17 G4
Bonehurst Rd. RH1 21 G6
Bourne Rd. RH1 17 E5
Bramble Clo. RH1 19 H5
*Bramble Walk,
　Bramble Clo. RH1 19 H5
Brambletye Park Rd. RH1 19 G6
Bramblewood. RH1 16 D4

Bramley Clo. RH1 19 F6
Brandsland. RH2 20 C2
Brightlands Rd. RH2 18 D2
Brighton Rd,
　Redhill. RH1 19 F5
Brighton Rd,
　Salfords. RH1 21 G5
Broadhurst Gdns. RH2 18 C6
Brokes Cres. RH2 18 B2
Brokes Rd. RH2 18 B2
Brook Rd,
　Merstham. RH1 17 E3
Brook Rd, Redhill. RH1 19 G4
Brookfield Clo. RH1 21 G3
Brooklands Ct. RH2 18 C2
Brooklands Way. RH1 19 F2
Brownlow Rd. RH1 19 E3
Buckhurst Clo. RH1 19 F2
Budgen Dri. RH1 19 G1
Burnham Dri. RH2 18 B3
Burwood Clo. RH1 18 D4
Bushetts Gro. RH1 16 D4
Bushfield Dri. RH1 21 H2

Caberfeigh. RH1 19 E3
Canada Av. RH1 21 G2
Canada Dri. RH1 21 H2
Canons Clo. RH2 18 A2
Carlton Green. RH1 16 A6
Carlton Rd. RH1 16 A6
Carrington Clo. RH1 19 F3
Cartmel Clo. RH1 19 E2
Castle Clo. RH2 20 C2
Castle Dri. RH2 20 B2
*Castle Walk,
　London Rd. RH1 18 B3
Castlefield Rd. RH2 18 B3
Cavendish Gdns. RH1 19 H3
Cavendish Rd. RH1 19 G3
Caxton Rise. RH1 19 H3
Cedar Clo. RH2 18 D6
Chaldon Clo. RH1 19 F6
Chanctonbury Chase. RH1 19 H4
Chapel Rd. RH1 19 G3
Charman Rd. RH1 19 F3
Chart La. RH2 18 C4
Chart Way. RH2 18 C3
Chartfield Rd. RH1 18 C4
Cherry Green Clo. RH1 19 H5
Chesterton Dri. RH1 17 G3
Chestnut Clo. RH1 19 H5
*Chestnut Mead,
　Oxford Rd. RH1 19 F3
Chilberton Dri. RH1 17 E5
Chilmark Gdns. RH1 17 G3
Chipstead Clo. RH1 19 G5
Church Ct. RH2 18 C3
Church Hill. RH1 17 E1
Church Rd. RH1 19 F5
Church Rd. RH2 18 B6
Church St. RH1 18 B4
Church Walk. RH2 18 C4
Churchfield Rd. RH1 18 A3
Claremont Rd. RH1 16 C6
Clarence Rd. RH1 18 D6
Clarence Walk. RH1 19 E6
Clarendon Rd. RH1 19 E6
Clarendon Rd Sth. RH1 19 G2
Clayhall La. RH2 18 A6
Cleeves Ct. RH1 19 G2
Clyde Clo. RH1 19 H3
Cockshill Hill. RH2 18 C5
Cockshot Rd. RH2 18 C5
Colebrook Rd. RH1 19 F2
Colesmead Rd. RH1 16 B5
College Cres. RH1 16 D6
Colley Way. RH2 18 A1
Colman Way. RH1 16 A6
Common Rd. RH1 19 F6
Coneyberry Rd. RH2 20 D2
Conifer Clo. RH2 18 B2
Coniston Way. RH2 19 E2
Copley Clo. RH1 19 F1
Coppice La. RH2 18 A2
Copse Rd. RH1 18 D6
Copsleigh Av. RH1 21 G5
Copsleigh Clo. RH1 21 G4
Copsleigh Way. RH1 21 G4
Cornfield Rd. RH2 18 D5
Cotland Acres. RH1 19 E6
Crakell Rd. RH2 18 D4
Cranston Clo. RH2 18 C5
Crescent Rd. RH2 18 B6
Cromwell Rd. RH1 19 G3
Cronks Hill. RH1 18 D5
Cronks Hill Clo. RH1 19 E6
Cronks Hill Rd. RH1 19 E5

Crossland Rd. RH1 19 H
Crossways La. RH1 16 A
Croydon Rd. RH2 18 C
Daneshill. RH1 19 F
Daneshill Clo. RH1 19 F
Deans Rd. RH1 17 E
Deerings Rd. RH2 18 C
Delabole Rd. RH1 17 G
Delamere Rd. RH2 20 C
Dennis Clo. RH1 19 F
Denton Rd. RH1 21 G
Devon Cres. RH1 19 E
Devon Rd. RH1 17 E
Diamond Ct. RH1 19 H
Dome Way. RH1 19 F
Doods Park Rd. RH2 18 C
Doods Rd. RH2 18 D
Doods Way. RH2 19 E
Doran Dri. RH1 19 E
Douglas Rd. RH2 18 C
Dovers Green Rd. RH2 20 C
Downswood. RH1 16 A
Duncroft Clo. RH2 18 A
Dundrey Cres. RH1 17 G
Dunlin Clo. RH1 21 F
Dunottar Clo. RH1 19 E
Dunraven Av. RH1 21 H
Durfold Dri. RH2 18 C

Earlsbrook Rd. RH1 19 G
Earlswood Rd. RH1 19 F
East Rd. RH2 18 A
East Walk. RH2 18 C
Eastnor Rd. RH2 18 E
Edgefield Clo. RH1 21 H
Effingham Rd. RH2 18 C
Eldersley Clo. RH1 19 H
Eldersley Gdns. RH1 19 H
Elm Rd. RH1 19 H
Elmwood Rd. RH1 16 D
Emlyn Rd. RH1 19 C
Endsleigh Rd. RH1 17 H
Eversfield Rd. RH2 18 C
Evesham Clo. RH2 18 A
Evesham Rd. RH2 18 A
Evesham Rd Nth. RH2 18 A

Fairfax Av. RH1 19 H
Fairford Clo. RH2 18 D
Fairhaven Rd. RH1 16 C
Fairlawn Dri. RH1 19 H
Felland Way. RH2 20 D
Feltham Rd. RH1 21 H
Feltham Walk. RH1 21 H
Fengates Rd. RH1 19
Fenton Clo. RH1 19 C
Fenton Rd. RH1 19 C
Fir Tree Walk. RH2 18 H
Flint Clo. RH1 19
Fountain Rd. RH1 19
Foxley Clo. RH1 21 H
Frenches. RH1 19 C
Frenches Ct. RH1 19
Frenches Rd. RH1 16 H
Friths Dri. RH2 18
Fulbourne Clo. RH1 19
Furze Clo. RH1 19
Furze Hill. RH1 19
Furzefield Cres. RH2 18 H
Furzefield Rd. RH2 18 H

Gable Ct. RH1 19 H
Garibaldi Rd. RH1 19
Garlands Rd. RH1 19
Gatton Bottom. RH1 16
Gatton Clo. RH2 18
Gatton Park Rd. RH1 16
Gatton Rd. RH2 18 A
Gloucester Rd. RH1 19
Glovers Rd. RH2 18
Goodwood Rd. RH1 19
Gordon Rd. RH1 19
Grange Clo. RH1 16
Grange Dri. RH1 17
Grantwood Clo. RH1 21
Green La, Redhill. RH1 19
Green La, Reigate. RH2 18
Green La,
　White Bushes. RH1 21
Green Way. RH1 19
Greenhayes Clo. RH2 18
Greensan Clo. RH1 17
Greenwood Dri. RH1 21
Greystones Clo. RH1 18
Greystones Dri. RH2 18
Grosvenor Mews. RH2 20
Grovehill Rd. RH1 19